AD

ANTONELLVS·MESSA NESIS·P·

ICB .

BRONZO FIORENTINO

Ant° van Dyck·fecit·

FH

Renoir

Gio·Antonio Guardi f.

HG .

A: 1611.

iB·Greuze

ICB

ÆME·IXH·XÆN

15IZ

IOANNES BELLINVS·P·

Rembrandt f
1634

MCS

GREAT DRAWINGS OF THE MASTERS

GREAT DRAWINGS

OF THE

MASTERS

———

EDITED AND SELECTED BY

J. E. SCHULER

TEXT BY

DR. ROLF HÄNSLER

G. P. PUTNAM'S SONS

NEW YORK

FIRST AMERICAN EDITION
Translated from the German by Gillian Brydone
First published in Germany in 1962 as
MEISTERZEICHNUNGEN VON DER WELT BEWUNDERT
by Schuler Verlagsgesellschaft, Stuttgart
Copyright © 1962 Schuler Verlagsgesellschaft, Stuttgart
Library of Congress Catalog Card Number: 63–12754
Printed in West Germany

CONTENTS

We acknowledge gratefully the co-operation of the following museums, art galleries and collections to which the original drawings belong for permission to reproduce them here

THE NATURE OF THE DRAWING

For centuries an interest in drawings was the privilege of scholars, artists and dilettantes alone. Only in the last few decades have drawings attracted a wider circle of art-lovers. It is typical of our modern attitude to art that we no longer consider the height of artistic achievement to lie only in the "finished" work. We are eager to trace the process of creation back to its very beginnings. When the Impressionists held their first exhibition they were accused of not working out their paintings to the last naturalistic detail, and therefore of not "completing" them, in the sense in which the Renaissance painters "completed" their work. But it was just this unfinished quality that opened the door for later generations, enabling them to delve deeper into the spontaneous creative process that leads up to a work of art by way of the drawing. Here, in the sketch, study or preliminary draft, for all to see, lie the first inspirations, the first thoughts, the first impressions from life that determine the artist's intentions.

It would be hard for us fully to understand painters like Dürer, Grünewald, Michelangelo, Raphael, Elsheimer, Rembrandt, Goya or Toulouse-Lautrec, such is the complexity of their work, if we did not have a knowledge of their graphic skill, and particularly their draftsmanship. Fortunately a representative selection of these artists' drawings have been preserved for our enjoyment; with so many other masters, only a fragment here and there can be attributed to them, and then only after much difficult and specialized research.

It has become a common practice, especially since the big comprehensive exhibitions of the post-war years, to flank every artist's paintings with what is sometimes a considerable number of his drawings. The publication of drawings, too, in a form available to wide circles of readers has never – since the learned treatises of the eighteenth century in England and France – assumed such dimensions as today. It is also now easier than ever to see original works; anyone may visit one of the most important collections in the newly opened Queen's Gallery in Buckingham Palace; and the Department of Prints and Drawings in the British Museum, the collections in the Ashmolean Museum in Oxford, the Pierpont Morgan Library in America and the provincial museums of France, and the enormous reserves in the Hermitage in Leningrad are open to all. In addition, more and more private collectors are tending to give the public access to their treasures in special exhibitions. This custom is becoming increasingly widespread in England and America.

It was, above all, the collectors who laid the foundations of the science and lore of drawings. In the art of drawing, the tiniest mark can have the greatest significance. That is why, in the early days of drawing collections, it was first and foremost the artists who hastened to secure the works left at the death of their masters or their contemporaries. This was because they wanted either to take over a ready-made formula or to complete preliminary studies.

Austrian Master · 1320–1365   Albertina, Vienna

The first collections of sketches resulted from the need of the late medieval studies for material to copy. We know, for example, that it was not only as a young man that Dürer copied the themes of the painter he most admired, Schongauer, in order to absorb the latter's repertoire of motives and forms. When he was mature he also tried to obtain the drawings of contemporaries like Raphael and Jacopo de Barbari by bartering for them. The painter Vasari, the first artist-biographer in Europe in the middle of the sixteenth century, culled most of the material for his *Lives of the Most Eminent Architects, Painters and Sculptors of Italy* from his own massive collection of drawings. These he mounted himself and they are today the pride of many public collections. It is precisely from this period of the High Renaissance that we hear the first intimations that art-lovers were trying to acquire the sketches of the masters they admired. The stock of drawings left at Michelangelo's death occasioned bitter quarrels because both pupils and heirs were equally anxious to possess them. In fact, nearly four hundred years of vicissitudes were to pass before the wanderings of this important group of drawings came to an end. The same thing might well have happened to the drawings of Leonardo, Raphael or Grünewald, and did, in fact, happen to those of Dürer, since a large part of his bequest was stolen from the collections of the Austrian Imperial Palace and found its way to the Kunsthalle in Bremen, only to be shamefully destroyed in its hiding-place towards the end of the Second World War.

Particularly after the beginning of the seventeenth century the collecting of drawings was taken over more and more by knowledgeable amateurs – or speculators. The recorded numbers of their collections run into tens of thousands, though, of course, this does include many copies that would not stand the test of modern scholarship and analysis. But most important

Benozzo Gozzoli · 1420–1498   British Museum, London

of all, as early as the seventeenth century the ruling houses of Europe, especially those of France and England, and the Hapsburgs in Austria, had begun to buy up the entire legacies and collections of amateurs and dilettantes to add to their folios. Without the collection of Jabach, the Cologne banker, without the enthusiasm of Ferdinand von Tirol, Governor of the Netherlands, without Charles II, the Arundels and many others, the collections of the Louvre, the Albertina in Vienna and the British Museum would not today contain the undisputed cream of the world's most important master drawings.

But these basic accumulations of drawings did not come into their real glory until the eighteenth century – the century of the "deliberate" collector, of the dawn of scholarship and critical insight. Although earlier collectors like Cardinal Leopoldo de' Medici (1675), who took over the treasures of Vasari and Borghini, formed their collections chiefly around the works of their contemporaries, collecting in the eighteenth century began to assume a far more eclectic air – and certainly a more commercial one. The auction-sales of the collections of Crozat, Caylus or Mariette, one of the forefathers of our modern scientific approach to drawings, caused a real sensation! The collections of the painters Lawrence and Reynolds – whose stamped collector's mark still counts as a guarantee today – contained unbelievable riches; not to mention those of the Viennese Count Fries and Duke Albert of Sachsen-Teschen, who founded the famous Albertina Collection with a bequest of 23,660 drawings. At a time when no one else in the world was interested in late Gothic Art, Duke Albert managed to obtain from the West Imperial Palace the remaining Dürer drawings that had reached the Court Library through Pirckheimer and Imhoff. They became the pride of the now public gallery in Vienna.

Hans Holbein the Elder · 1470–1524   Staedel Institute, Frankfurt

If the eighteenth century was the age of the amateur and the aristocratic collector, then the nineteenth belongs to the dealer and the scholar. The time for rational, critical discrimination had come. The number of enthusiasts, however, was still comparatively small. Private collections came and went without much ceremony. The beneficiaries were usually the big public galleries who could thus increase their stocks at little expense. Only a memory remains of names like Esdail, Warwick, Fries, Lanna, Goldschmidt and many others whose collections were scattered all over Europe by the big auctioneers. But there were at least two great collections that survived intact; Fairfax Murray's superb collection became the basis of the Pierpont Morgan Library in America; the Rhineland banker Koenig left his unique treasures to the Boymans – van Beuningen Museum in Rotterdam. Other collections have been broken up during the last decades, as for instance, that of Harry Oppenheimer, the London banker, who made the last private attempt at comprehensive representation, or the more traditionally selective collections of the Princes of Liechtenstein and the Princes of Arenberg which were scattered to the four winds in private deals, incidentally giving considerable impetus to speculation in art.

In spite of the fact that the best of the harvest has been reaped by public institutions and that comprehensive new collections are practically unthinkable, unless limited in period or extent, drawings are being collected all over the world as keenly as ever. The appeal of this shy peep into the artist's intuitive processes will always lead many people to prefer the working drawing, the first sketch or the study to the ultimate painting or sculpture – quite apart from the fact that the finished work of art is usually much more expensive.

Today we owe much to the many private collectors all over the world. It is due to their

Michelangelo · 1475–1564   Offizi Galeria, Florence

initiative that even in this over-commercialized and materialistic age collections of consider-able individual merit are still being formed.

More clearly than the painting, the drawing permits us to gain insight into the artist's first and perhaps most revealing concept of his work, for not every draftsman always intended to leave his drawings to posterity as a permanent evidence to his skill. The drawing in the late Middle Ages was usually a preparatory study, design or quick sketch for a fresco, mosaic, altar-piece, portrait or illuminated manuscript. This is one of the reasons why drawings have only been preserved since about the middle of the fourteenth century.

With so few opportunities of creating major works of their own, the imaginative develop-ment of many of these early artists was severely hampered. They did little else except repro-duce material that was passed on from studio to studio in the form of so-called "pattern-books." In the monastery schools, scriptoria and altar workshops everything that turned up was copied – but only with a view to future use. It is easy to understand why so few of these sketches have survived, since their quality is usually vastly inferior to that of the finished painting. Anything that by chance has been preserved makes it obvious that original forms and compositions were rare. For every subject a prescribed method of treatment was handed down from master to pupil. In simple outlines stressed by occasional thicker or blacker lines they depicted almost exclusively the biblical themes that were considered essential to the ecclesiastical art of the late Middle Ages.

A definite turning-point was reached towards the middle of the fifteenth century when man's feeling for nature began to awaken. Slowly artists started to free themselves from the restrictions of religious themes. Already their pictorial ideas were changing. The realism with

Il Ridotto vecchio · Francesco Guardi

Francesco Guardi · 1712–1793   Soviet Hermitage, Leningrad

which the Early Renaissance masters in Florence or the Van Eyck brothers rejoiced in the world around them came as a revelation to artists of other schools. The new perception was arousing the artist's desire to excel by his own personal imaginative efforts. In contrast to the impersonal character of Gothic Art, the drawings of the second half of the century were emphatically subjective and superbly individual. At last drawing had become an art in its own right, no longer a poor relation of painting.

After the Renaissance the drawing not only acquired technical perfection and freedom of choice in theme; it underwent a metamorphosis. The spiritualization of the subject-matter that was the aim of medieval artists resolved itself in a delight in visible, tangible beauty. In fact an age of spirituality was making way for an age of sensuality and a period which introduced the discovery of the nature of things. Thus man became the artist's chief preoccupation, either as a draped figure, a nude or a portrait. Affectionate and searching observation of human beings, plants, landscapes and man-made objects of all kinds evoked the desire and the ability to draw in perspective.

The re-discovery of linear perspective had the greatest impact on the new naturalistic perception. About the middle of the fifteenth century it conquered the art of drawing as well as its derivative Early Renaissance painting. This new perception was strongly stimulated, but certainly not caused, as was thought for a long time, by the re-discovery and excavation of antique monuments. For the first time in the history of art the drawing became an end in itself; as a collector's piece it was almost as sought after as the oil-painting.

It is easy to attribute drawings of this period to definite artists or schools; they always display an individual character even though they are often studies made for a set purpose. The

Francisco de Goya · 1746–1828   Museo National del Prado, Madrid

usual media are red and white chalk, silverpoint and charcoal. The evolution of the drawing continues uninterrupted throughout the succeeding centuries. It follows the mainstream of styles that supplant one another from the High Renaissance through Mannerism, Baroque, Classicism, Realism and Impressionism right up to the most recent movements.

It is beyond the scope of this brief preface to give an account of the art of drawing in the Western world. The notes to each plate provide sufficient indication of style and history. But at least a few remarks about the most important features of modern drawing will not be out of place.

The ideals of form in the works of the great artists of the nineteenth century up to the Impressionists were still those of the Renaissance and its disciples. Contours, modeling, light and shade, and especially the rules of linear perspective, determined the effect that the picture would have. In modern drawing, however, artists turned away from naturalism to express a more personal, inner world. The sense of perception and composition that was formerly determined by man's relationship to natural objects became more spontaneous. Artists adopted an astonishing directness of attack, an often nervous method of interpretation, strongly colored by the part played by the unconscious in the process of creation. Many artists sought that delightful naïvety that Ingres recommended to his pupils as the foundation of creative organization. As Kandinsky declared when referring to abstract art, the artist should view the natural objects around him as impenetrably mysterious and illusory. Nature should be replaced, after being assimilated and reshaped in the depths of the artist's soul, by rhythms and forms that are independent of Nature. Thus the drawing of our time is hardly ever an imitation or a copy. It is a kind of parable, the outward representative of an inward process,

Pablo Picasso · 1881–   Private Collection, Paris

even when it has been inspired by a concrete object. The courage to look at every external object as if seeing it for the first time, as Matisse insisted the artist should do, is as characteristic of the drawing in modern art as was the thesis propounded by Liebermann who astounded the academics of the old school by claiming that drawing was the art of omission.

The discovery of the expressive value of pure color by the Expressionists and Fauvists resulted in the drawing losing more and more of its significance as a preparatory study. But paradoxically this has only served to raise its value among collectors, whatever graphic technique has been employed, whether pure line drawing, quick sketch, etching, lithograph or any other. Today merit is judged more than ever in terms of the quality Paul Klee was describing in his "Farewell to the Past," when he said, "Art does not reproduce the visible; it reveals the visible."

PLATES

"*Johes De Eyck me fecit — 1437.*" So runs the inscription on the frame of this drawing which has been painted to imitate marble. Assuming that the signature is genuine, are we looking at the study for a picture that has disappeared or, as the precision suggests, a finished work? The dispute between the experts on this point will probably never be settled. Without doubt, however, this panel which was once attributed to Memling is an original work of incomparable merit. According to the legend, Saint Barbara was the daughter of the heathen lord Dioscuro, who tortured her to death. Unlike later masters who depicted her holding a symbolic temple tower, van Eyck has placed her in front of the tower of a Gothic cathedral with a book and martyr's palm in her hand. In the tracery of the building the artist has stressed a group of three windows. They are the symbols of Christianity that Barbara ordered the master-builders to insert, although her father had commissioned a temple with two windows. The hustle and bustle of a medieval building-site, where the pious are expiating their sins as unpaid labor, frames the noble figure of the martyr. In its dignity and solemnity this drawing is one of the most beautiful relics of medieval art in the Netherlands.

JAN VAN EYCK · SAINT BARBARA

(Maaseyck' near Maastricht c. 1390—1441 Bruges)
Saint Barbara · Dated 1437 · Brush on chalk ground,
on wood · 34,2 x 18,6 cm · Antwerp Museum

In the year 1432 the brothers Jan and Hubert van Eyck put the finishing touches to their Ghent altar. This marked the beginning of the history of Dutch art and northern post-medieval oil-painting. A year earlier the priest shown in this silverpoint drawing was residing in the Netherlands as an ambassador. He was Cardinal of S. Croce in Florence, and at that time fifty-six years old. This perceptive study is one of very few from the hand of van Eyck that remain. It was once thought to be only a copy of the master's first superb panel-painting, now in Vienna, which portrays the Cardinal. Today this drawing is generally accepted as being a study for the Vienna portrait. In its penetrating characterization, it is truly worthy of the great portraitist, van Eyck. With great economy of line, he has given his not immediately attractive model a compelling air of nobility.

JAN VAN EYCK · PORTRAIT OF CARDINAL
NICCOLO ALBERGATI

(Maaseyck' near Maastricht c. 1390—1441 Bruges)
Portrait of Cardinal Niccolo Albergati,
Archbishop of Bologna · 1431 · Silverpoint 21,4 x 18 cm
Dresden, Kupferstichkabinett

The creator of this vivid brush drawing was one of the few of Giotto's pupils whose work has been clearly established. He came from a distinguished, and later, very wealthy Florentine family out of which several scholars, statesmen, cardinals and literati emerged during the fifteenth century. This drawing with its imaginative Gothic architecture set off against a dark blue sky, is a study for a series of twelve authentic frescoes illustrating scenes from the life of the Virgin Mary. Gaddi has shown the scene, in accordance with contemporary religious symbolism, on a stairway; an early attempt to bring persons and places into harmony. At the same time, however, the figures float rather than stand, and the rules of linear perspective have not been followed. This shows us how strongly the artist was affected by the spirit of Gothic art, to which naturalistic spatial organization was still completely alien.

TADDEO GADDI
PURIFICATION OF THE VIRGIN MARY

*(Florence c. 1300—1366) · Purification of the Virgin Mary
(Study for the fresco in the Baronvelli Chapel
in S. Croce in Florence) · Pen heightened with white on
green prepared paper · 36 x 28,5 cm · Paris, Louvre*

In contrast to the clear lines and modeling of the nudes he usually draws, Pisanello is here attempting to give an impression of texture and color. Although still restricted to the traditional profile position of the heads and still fumbling for stability in the figures, the artist has certainly attained a high degree of artistry in this simple costume study. By means of pen and wash, a daring combination at the time, he has managed to capture the allure of the several different materials in the costumes. This achievement gave him great influence over his contemporaries. As in the case of many artists in the early days of drawing, Pisanello's position is based more on his draftmanship than on his panel-paintings.

ANTONIO PISANO, PISANELLO
MAN AND WOMAN IN PERIOD COSTUME

(Verona c. 1397—1455 Rome) · Man and Woman in Period Costume · Pen and red, brown and green water-color · 27,2 x 18,9 cm · Chantilly, Musée Condé

This sheet of studies dates from the early days of draftsmanship in Europe. It is particularly fortunate that it has been preserved because panels and frescoes of that period were almost always painted from pattern-books. At the same time is constitutes one of the oldest examples of nude poses. These are rare because of bitter opposition from the Church. To Pisanello, however, everything in nature was material for his analytical eye. He gave a strong impetus to Italian medal-engraving and practically discovered zoological and botanical drawing. In the sketches shown here he was striving to unveil the principles of feminine beauty, just as Dürer was to do. Using confident outlines and soft modeling, Pisanello attacked and solved the problems of "standing" and "walking." How far ahead of his times he was in this is shown by the conventional kneeling angel in the upper half of the sheet whose pose is still completely determined by the folds of his garments.

ANTONIO PISANO, PISANELLO
SHEET OF STUDIES OF FEMALE NUDES

(Verona c. 1397—1455 Rome) · Sheet of Studies of Female Nudes · Pen and brown ink on parchment 22,2 x 16,6 cm · Rotterdam, Boymans-van Beuningen Museum

This intelligent-looking head dates from the early years of French panel-painting. Fouquet started his career as a miniature-painter and enamellist. As early as 1437, although still very young, he spent some time in Rome and even painted the portrait of Pope Eugene IV. He based his technique on that of the van Eyck brothers but was intellectually far beyond any other of their disciples. In 1460 he painted the famous forty miniatures for the Book of Hours of Etienne Chevalier, the Royal Chamberlain. They are kept in the Musée Condé in Chantilly as part of the French National Treasure. Nervous lines, sharply defined forms and a deep understanding of humanity distinguish the work of this artist from the Loire. With a sober, objective touch he endowed the model with an air of nobility of soul and intellectual supremacy, reminiscent of the effect achieved by both Holbein and Dürer. A portrait like this is, graphically, an astonishing feat, especially when we remember that this "peintre du roy" died while Dürer was still a boy.

JEAN FOUQUET
PORTRAIT OF A PRIEST

(Tours c. 1420—1477/81) · Portrait of a Priest · C. 1460
Silverpoint on ivory tinted paper · 19,5 x 13 cm
New York, Metropolitan Museum of Art

Uccello, whose real name was Paolo di Dono, was born in Florence. After starting his career in the Gothic school, he became so fascinated by the so-called "modern" realism of Masaccio and Donatello that he, too, turned to lifelike studies of nature, and continuous searching for new methods of interpretation. Vasari relates that he gave much thought to the problems of perspective which were preoccupying every artist at the time, but which had not yet been co-ordinated into a theory. Thus Uccello became one of the generation of Florentine "systematizers." This galloping horse has been captured with a confident outline and is depicted with a strength that appears again only in a study for a memorial by Leonardo. The drawing gives ample proof of Uccello's unusual gift for the grandiose.

PAOLO DI DONO, UCCELLO
SAINT GEORGE

(Florence 1397—1475) · Saint George
Pen and silverpoint heightened with white on turquoise colored paper · 30 x 33 cm · Florence, Uffizi

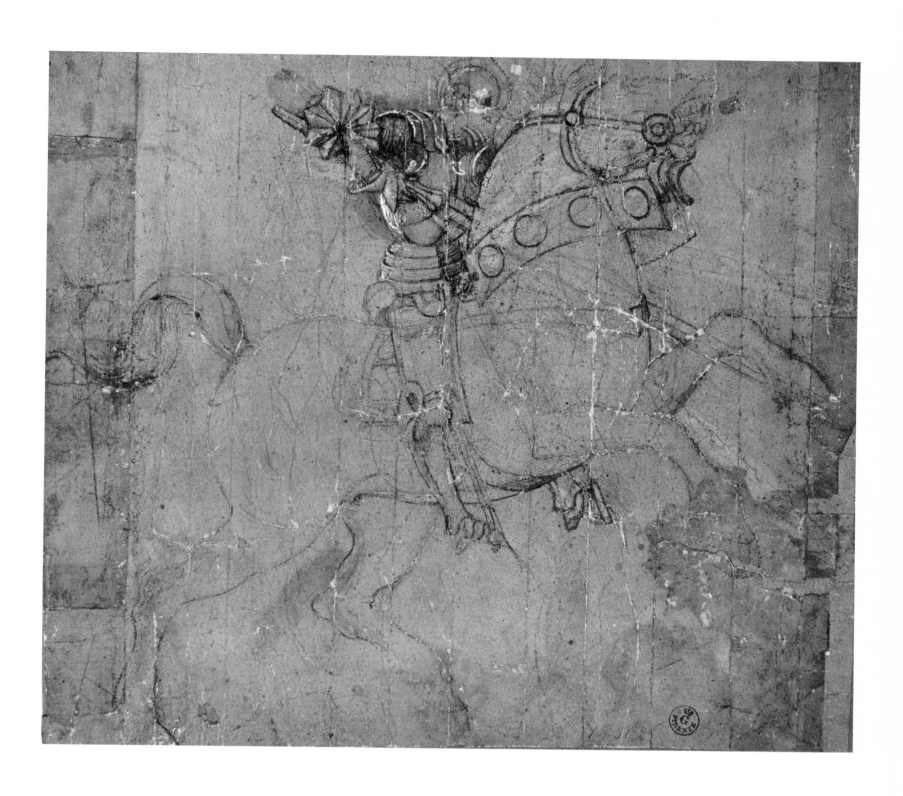

The historical importance of the creator of this unusual scene is due to his influence as a teacher in the second half of the fifteenth century. Goldsmiths and sculptor-painters such as the brothers Pollaiuolo and also Ghirlandaio, Michelangelo's teacher, studied under him. Baldovinetti, few of whose paintings have been preserved, deserves much credit for the varnishing technique which he used even on his frescoes. In addition he worked in mosaic, and among other things restored the mosaics in S. Miniato al Monte and the baptistry in Florence. That he retained an alert eye for everyday scenes in spite of all these religious commissions is shown by this sketch which he must have jotted down in the street. The two young gallants are astonishingly lifelike in pose and gesture, giving an example of free graphic story-telling rarely seen in a century from which so few drawings have survived.

ALESSO BALDOVINETTI
TWO YOUTHS PAYING COURT TO A LADY

(Florence 1425—1499) · Two Youths Paying Court to a Lady (detail) · Pen and wash · 11,6 x 12,8 cm Florence, Uffizi

Panicale

Antonello's portraits and altar-paintings caused a furore in Northern Italy. With their help Venice caught up with the lead that Florence, cradle of the Early Renaissance, had won during the first half of the fifteenth century. In fact Vasari even credits Antonello with the introduction of oil-painting into Venice. This drawing demonstrates how the artist deviated from the rigid profile poses of the Florentine and Lombard masters. It shows the face of a boy in three-quarter profile, a new pose which soon became fashionable. This fine head also has hair cut in a fringe, one of the features of all Antonello's paintings. It has been superbly executed with the ubiquitous silverpoint. Unfortunately, very little is known about Antonello's life. In the early days of scholarship, however, it was established that he had an influence on Giovanni Bellini and his school, and introduced new methods of drawing and painting, a fact which ensures his fame in spite of the obscurity that surrounds him.

ANTONELLO DA MESSINA
HEAD OF A BOY

(Messina c. 1430—1479) · Head of a Boy
Black chalk · 33 x 26,9 cm · Vienna, Albertina

This early Venetian sketch displays an accurate, subtle, but almost disembodied delicacy of line. Like all silverpoint drawings at a time when the pencil was unknown, it was not created as an end in itself, but more likely as the study for a larger composition. Hence the fortuitous nature of the sheet and the unusual arrangement of the planes. In contrast to the fine hatching usual in the North, this masterpiece gains its sculptural quality from chalk highlights, which gave excellent effects on the tinted paper that had just reached Venice. It is by Bellini, Titian's master, and is unfortunately very badly preserved. Indeed, few but Bellini could have drawn a face of such expressive beauty, which perhaps explains why Dürer, on his second visit to Italy, was more impressed by Bellini's work than any other, and also why he assimilated so much of the latter's classicism.

GIOVANNI BELLINI
PORTRAIT HEAD OF A YOUNG WOMAN

*(Venice c. 1430—1510) · Portrait Head of a Young Woman
Silverpoint heightened with white on green-gray
tinted paper · 20,8 x 13,8 cm · Venice, Accademia*

If the historical concept "Renaissance" really has the meaning of "rebirth" — the rebirth of classical art — then it is closely applicable to this work by the greatest graphic artist and most interesting painter of the fifteenth century in Northern Italy. Treading as gracefully as Botticelli's maidens, this figure seems to be inspired by the Panathenaean frieze on the pediment of the Parthenon, proof enough that Mantegna was pursuing the same ideals in his studies as his Tuscan contemporaries, the second generation of Florentine artists. Like them he steeped himself in the principles of form embodied in the Greek works of art that were being imported into Italy, usually at the behest of some collector. In 1460 he took up his appointment to the Gonzaga court in Mantua, where he died, forty-six years later. Mantegna belonged to those artists who made a decisive break with Byzantine and Gothic principles of composition and concentrated on the naturalistic figures and spatial relationships supposed to have been re-discovered in Hellenic sculpture.

ANDREA DEL MANTEGNA
DANCING MUSE FROM "PARNASSUS"

(Isola di Carturo near Padua 1431—1506 Mantua)
Dancing Muse from "Parnassus" · C. 1497
Pen and wash heightened with white · 52 x 25,9 cm
Munich, Staatliche Graphische Collection

The Medici brothers' beautiful and noble sarcophagus in the old sacristy in Florence and the majestic equestrian memorial to the warrior Colleoni alone would have sufficed to ensure Verrocchio undying fame as a sculptor. As a pupil of Baldovinetti he exerted great influence on Early Renaissance art in Tuscany. He himself had several pupils such as Botticini, Lorenzo di Credi and, most important of all, Leonardo da Vinci. In fact Lorenzo left his earliest masterpiece, a kneeling angel, in Verrocchio's famous "Baptism of Christ," now in the Accademia in Florence. A glance at the eyes and mouth of the study reproduced here shows how the artist has used a suggestive distribution of light and sculptured modeling to achieve a beauty and depth of expression that are strongly reminiscent of Leonardo. Verrocchio's sensitive portraits and Madonnas hang in galleries in London, Berlin and Frankfurt.

ANDREA DEL VERROCCHIO
HEAD OF AN ANGEL

(Florence 1436—1488) · Head of an Angel · C. 1475
Charcoal and brush · 21 x 18,3 cm · Florence, Uffizi

During the Gothic period human figures were always drawn as if floating above the earth. This youth who stands so firmly on both feet is the result of a development in the power of perception that originated with Giotto. After the first masters of the Early Renaissance in Florence, Masaccio, Masolino and Mantegna, it was Signorelli, head of the Umbrian-Tuscan School, who contributed most to the stabilization of the human figure. Some time after 1470 Signorelli joined Verrocchio's circle in Florence and between 1499 and 1506 he painted his chief work, the inspired "Last Judgment" scenes in the Orvieto Cathedral. This made him the first painter of nudes in Italian art. This study of a sturdy fencer displays his feeling for uncomplicated shapes. It also shows how he gradually merged several light, searching lines into a solid form — for example, the youth's left arm and legs.

LUCA SIGNORELLI · FIGURE OF A YOUTH

(Cortona 1441—1523) · Figure of a Youth · C. 1500
Charcoal · 25 x 17 cm · Florence, Uffizi

Sandro Filipepi was nicknamed "il Botticelli," the "little barrel," because of his tubby figure, while still a boy. He studied under that jovial Bohemian, Fra Filippo Lippi. As sensitive as Lippi, but more versatile and earnest, Botticelli was the "poet" of the fifteenth century masters. He created sometimes gracious Madonnas, sometimes elegant figures from Greek mythology, but always with the idea of glorifying feminine beauty. A classical sense of beauty and a Gothic sense of line were united in his work to sing a hymn to terrestrial happiness. After he was forty, depression caused by the burning of Savonarola made Botticelli destroy all his non-religious works. In this drawing, one of the few that have survived, the artist has treated the light-footed maiden's robes with such delicacy that he gives the effect of nudity. Followed by two of the Putti which first appeared in Donatello's and Verrocchio's sculptures, she carries a cornucopia full of fruit symbolizing the blessings of Nature.

ALESSANDRO FILIPEPI,
SANDRO BOTTICELLI
ABUNDANCE OR AUTUMN

*(Florence 1444/5—1510) · Abundance or Autumn
C. 1485 · Pen and bister and wash heightened with white
on colored paper · 31,5 x 25,5 cm
London, British Museum*

What a strange drawing this is for a Florentine painter in an age that was intoxicated by beauty! To frame this horribly deformed face with a decorative oval and a quartet of beautiful nymphs! It has been deduced that this drawing is a self-portrait of Ghirlandaio who, as a young man, won much fame and riches by designing and fashioning "ghirlandi," a kind of hair-ornament, for the ladies of Florence. It is more important for us today that the artist has given this un-rivaled drawing such an intensely human content. He has imbued the old man's pitiable face with dignity, bitterness and resignation. This drawing surpasses even the moving portrait of the same subject in the Louvre that shows him as a loving grandfather with his grandchild. It is even more significant that Ghirlandaio, leading panel and fresco painter of the last part of the fifteenth century, should have been both Baldovinetti's pupil and, later, the master of Leonardo.

DOMENICO GHIRLANDAIO
PORTRAIT OF AN OLD MAN

(Florence 1449—1494) · Portrait of an Old Man
Silverpoint heightened with white · 29,5 x 34 cm
Stockholm, National Museum

About 1500 in Italy, as in the works of Albrecht Altdorfer, in Germany, religious themes were ceasing to dominate every picture and landscape was coming to the fore. This development eventually led to the landscape as such. At the same time this drawing shows how lovingly Florentine fifteenth-century masters steeped themselves in Nature and constructed their imaginary landscapes out of many isolated observations. The legend of the hermit Jerome, who went to do penance in the wilderness, was only an excuse for Piero to display his personal talent for rugged landscape. But his feeling for Nature, in Dürer's sense of the word, lagged behind his power of imaginative scenic composition. Piero was a younger contemporary of Leonardo and Botticelli and owes much to them.

PIERO DI COSIMO
ST. JEROME DOING PENANCE

(Florence 1462—1521) · St. Jerome Doing Penance C. 1510 · Pen · 23,5 x 20 cm · Florence, Uffizi

Without a halo, earth-bound, almost bourgeois, this Virgin and Child has been depicted according to late fifteenth-century taste. Only the play on the symbolic flower, a motif popular even before this time, and the late Gothic-Mannerist treatment of the folds on the flowing cloak betray the religious inspiration behind this deeply felt drawing. In some of the curves and convolutions of the cloak there is a hint of the auricular style of German Renaissance sculpture. Schongauer's studies of this kind had a far-reaching influence. His graphic art was admired and imitated even in Italy. Techniques like cross-hatching, the occasional black patches and, above all, the light effects on the Virgin's hair, her dress and the flower-pot, were pioneer work in those days, not becoming general practice until after the death of Dürer.

MARTIN SCHONGAUER
MADONNA ON A GRASS BANK
WITH A CARNATION PLANT

*(Colmar c. 1445—1491 Breisach) · Madonna
on a Grass Bank with a Carnation Plant · C. 1480
Pen and brown ink · 22,7 x 15,9 cm
Berlin, Kupferstichkabinett*

The discovery of several frescoes during the restoration of Breisach Cathedral after the war has raised Schongauer, the painter of the "Madonna in the Rosebush," even higher than ever before in scholarly estimation. In this warm, lively angel's head we notice mostly the pleasure he took in the linear treatment of the hair. To try and give an effect of light and shade by drawing waves and ringlets in strokes of varying strengths was a new departure for those days, when artists were still thinking in terms of outlines. But countless masters adopted the new techniques. Although Schongauer was still moving hesitantly toward facial modeling with his parallel lines, he had already achieved full mastery of sweeping contours as exemplified by this expressive face, with its sculptured eyelids and pupils and animated mouth.

MARTIN SCHONGAUER · ANGEL'S HEAD

(Colmar c. 1445—1491 Breisach) · Angel's Head
Pen and brown ink · 13 x 10,8 cm
Munich, Staatliche Graphische Collection

With its clear outlines thrown into relief by hatching and cross-hatching, heightened with white, this delightful leaf is one of the loveliest things that has been preserved from the early years of German drawing. The motif of a couple riding on one horse was very popular in those days. Albrecht Dürer also used it in a drawing that dates from 1489. Finely observed in detail, expressed with the utmost grace, this drawing may well have been one of those independent works that were already being collected by connoisseurs. On the other hand it may have been a study for a larger work, such as a mural. The fluttering banners must have been designed to carry a verse from some medieval love song.

NUREMBERG MASTER
COUPLE ON HORSEBACK

Couple on Horseback · C. 1470/80
Pen and black ink heightened with white on olive-green tinted paper · 19,8 x 15,5 cm · Formerly in Vienna, Graf Lanckoronski Collection

Subtle simplicity, accurate characterization and economical, almost unshaded outlines typify the style of the anonymous artist who is known as the "Meister des Hausbuchs" and who still puzzles the scholars. The name is due to a series of brilliant drawings that show daily life in the late Middle Ages. This sketch is one of sixty drawings known to be his work, although the unlikely date was probably added later. It shows a moment of delightful feminine charm and masculine impudence, a foretaste of the scenes from the lives of peasants and townsfolk in castles, alleyways and gardens and even in the Imperial Court of Maximilian in Bruges, which the unknown master depicted with all the zest of a raconteur. His style and technique had a considerable influence on such artists as Dürer, Baldung and Grünewald in South Germany, and Rembrandt in Holland.

MEISTER DES HAUSBUCHS
YOUNG COUPLE STANDING

*(fl. c. 1475—1490) · Young Couple Standing
Silverpoint on white prepared paper · 19,6 x 13,5 cm
Berlin, Kupferstichkabinett*

The idea of presenting a tree as a human being could only have occurred to a Northern artist with an imagination that dared to roam beyond the actual and the visible. In fact this Dutchman used his finely differentiated pen-strokes to produce "surrealist" drawings centuries before this method of taking dreams seriously was hailed as a movement in art. In this drawing he gave a ludicrous figment of his imagination boats for feet, and set it in one of his endless land-scapes like a Gargantuan tramp, used and abused by man and animal, both pitiable and ridiculous at the same time. Bosch — his real name was Hieronymus van Acken, but he renamed himself, probably after his native town, 's Hertogenbosch — also decorated religious panels with the fantastic creations of his mind. The influence of the terrifying, moralizing and entertaining aspects of his completely personal art can be traced right up to the latter end of the sixteenth century.

HIERONYMUS BOSCH · THE TREE-MAN

('s Hertogenbosch c. 1450 — c. 1516) · The Tree-Man
Pen and bister · 27,7 x 21,1 cm · Vienna, Albertina

This portrait was drawn in the period after Dürer's second journey to Italy (1505—1507), and probably depicts a young girl from Nuremberg. In the powerful, expressive lines of the face, the eyebrows, the mouth and the collar we recognize Dürer's heritage of German Gothic. In the modeling of the head and particularly in the sublime calm and spirituality of the expression, we are conscious of a sense of harmony obviously deriving from his stay in Venice. This last influence manifested itself throughout the second half of his life in purified but less dynamic masterpieces. Since Dürer, so quickly famous, made a habit of signing his sketches, a large portion of them have been preserved, in spite of the fact that, when on his travels in the Netherlands (1520—1521), he recorded that he drew them as gifts in return for hospitality.

ALBRECHT DÜRER · PORTRAIT OF A GIRL

(Nuremberg 1471—1528) · Portrait of a Girl
Charcoal · 42,5 x 29,5 cm · Stockholm, National Museum

Dürer spent almost a year of his time in the Netherlands, from summer 1520 to spring 1521, in Antwerp, the "Antorff" of his diaries. With a tirelessly observant eye he sketched and noted everything he saw. At the same time he associated with people from every walk of life, and was welcomed everywhere as the famous German artist. This clearly constructed view of the banks of the Schelde is a rare document for its time. It shows a completely new understanding of the outside world. The horizon is exactly in the center of the picture. It brings out the towers and fortifications of the town walls on the right side, while the accentuated diagonal line of the quays, and the row of boats with their tall masts, leads from the foreground back into the depths of the picture. This diagonal line divides the sketch, because of the emptiness of sky and harbor, into two large, impressive spaces. This is just one example of the way in which Dürer turned a momentary visual experience into a spontaneous masterpiece.

ALBRECHT DÜRER
LANDING PLACE BY SCHELDE GATE
IN ANTWERP

(Nuremberg 1471—1528) · Landing Place by the Schelde Gate in Antwerp (fragment) · 1520 · Pen and ink 21,3 x 28,3 cm · Vienna, Albertina

A romantic landscape, luxuriant foliage, a story told with all the warmth and feeling of a troubadour — this is a striking variation on the theme of true love. It is difficult to tell which quality of this drawing is the most truly German. Is it the technique itself, with its subtle lines that curl and flare, the lighting effects in the trees, the composition of background and foreground or the expressive treatment of the lovers? The master from Kronach belongs with Dürer among the greatest figures of the time of the Reformation. He was also a friend of Martin Luther. It is true that much of his inspiration derives from Dürer's work, but he still gave his own naïve and very personal touch to his joyful masterpieces.

LUCAS CRANACH THE ELDER
LOVERS IN A LANDSCAPE

*(Kronach 1472—1553 Weimar) · Lovers in a Landscape
C. 1505 · Pen and bister · 28,2 x 20,6 cm
Berlin, Kupferstichkabinett*

In 1537 Cranach the Elder, overburdened by his triple career as mayor, apothecary and book-printer, handed over the direction of his large workshop to his second son, Lucas. Because of this, many studio paintings were produced that cannot be accurately attributed owing to their uniform signature. No one would deny today, however, that Cranach's son was an important portrait-painter who ranked high above his provincial successors. This gracious and delicate portrait of a princess "à la mode" is almost French in its sensitivity and charm and reminds us of the work of Clouet. It is not only one of the best sixteenth-century studies but also one of the most beautiful examples of work from the studio of the founder of the Protestant school of painting in Saxony. In the soft modeling of the face the younger Cranach betrays the influence of the Madonnas, Lucrecias and Venuses with which his father ornamented the German courts.

LUCAS CRANACH THE YOUNGER
PORTRAIT OF PRINCESS ELIZABETH
OF SAXONY

(Wittenberg 1515—1586 Weimar) · Portrait of
Princess Elizabeth of Saxony · C. 1555 · Brush, brown ink
and oil-paint on pink tinted paper · 38,7 x 28,3 cm
Berlin, Kupferstichkabinett

A fantastic apparition of macabre demonism, a grim frolic, this drawing conjures up the wild romanticism of the witches' kitchen and of the Blockberg scene in Goethe's "Faust." Baldung was a pupil of Dürer and the artist of the masterly High Altar in Freiburg Cathedral. For his time, he showed an astonishing capacity to use the female nude in almost surrealistic compositions, whereas other artists saw it only in terms of a "hymn to beauty." His sure knowledge of human anatomy, skill and clear spatial presentation approach the technical brilliance of the great Dürer. This scene possesses some of the strength and fury of Dante's poetry; it is one of the most exciting works by this Alsatian artist of Swabian origin. Baldung used the same theme in a woodcut dated 1510.

HANS BALDUNG-GRIEN
WITCHES' SABBATH II

(Schwäbisch Gmünd, c. 1484/85—1545 Strasburg)
Witches' Sabbath II · 1514 · Pen heightened with white
on red-brown tinted paper · 28,7 x 20,6 cm
Vienna, Albertina

Altdorfer was one of the most important masters of the Danube School and painted the first German landscape without figures, the so-called Munich "Woodland Scene." In this drawing he has made full use of his vivid imagination to illustrate the legend of Susanna in the grounds of a magnificent palace. As always in his work, the story is subordinate to its setting. Dramatic descriptions were alien to the visionary nature of this artist, but he compensated by reproducing the structural beauty of the buildings and park in the minutest detail so that, as in the completed painting, they make a far greater impact than the scene in the foreground. Again, as in the painting, it is difficult to pick out the two Elders, whose punishment, though still to follow, is being meted out on the terraces of the palace. Altdorfer's homely clumps of trees and bushes, as in the left of the picture, influenced later artists like Wolf Huber, Augustin Hirschvogel and Hans Lautensack, and gave a considerable stimulus to the development of landscape painting in Germany.

ALBRECHT ALTDORFER
SUSANNA IN THE BATH

*(Regensburg c. 1480—1538) · Susanna in the Bath
C. 1526 · (Study for the painting in the old Pinakothek, Munich) · Pen and blackish brown ink · 33,2 x 27,4 cm
Düsseldorf, Städtische Kunstsammlungen*

Huber, now considered as a member of the Danube School that centered around Altdorfer, was giving a highly personal account of his fiery temperament when he conceived this unconstrained landscape. According to the Evangelists, this scene occurred during Christ's last days on earth in a garden just outside the gates of Jerusalem, where many olive trees grew. In his acute sensitivity, however, Huber was so deeply involved in the spiritual content of the story that he invented botanically unclassifiable trees instead, endowing them with the power to share in the Savior's agonies. The romanticism of this alpine landscape, the tower that indicates the Gethsemane courtyard, the flaming grove and the dramatic characterization of the foreground bring this leaf near to the artistic standards of a Grünewald.

WOLF HUBER · CHRIST IN GETHSEMANE

*(Feldkirch c. 1490—1553 Passau) · Christ in Gethsemane
C. 1518 · Pen and brush in black heightened with white on
red tinted paper · 28,2 x 19,8 cm
Berlin, Kupferstichkabinett*

This study for one wing of an altar-piece was intended to give the effect of a sculpture. Although it was drawn a considerable time after Grünewald's famous panels for Dürer's Heller altar in Aschaffenburg, it shows the same pleated effect in the folds, the same specifically Grünewald poise of the head and the strong emphasis on lighting that one notices in his painted panels in Frankfurt and Donaueschingen. Even the saint's sculpture-like position on the daïs is to be seen in several of his works. It places Grünewald at the stylistic level of late Gothic. This figure, far removed from the idealism of Dürer or Holbein, expresses much of the ardent religious zeal which, in an age of violent mental tensions, so often turned the act of artistic creation to an outburst of spiritual protest.

MATTHIAS GRÜNEWALD
SAINT DOROTHY

(Würzburg c. 1460—1528 Halle) · Saint Dorothy
C. 1520 · Black chalk and India ink heightened with white
35,8 x 25,6 cm · Berlin, Kupferstichkabinett

The secret of the younger Holbein's consummate portraiture lies in a superb technique and a method of expression which enabled him to become a part of every one of his models. Growing up between the Augsburg and Ulm traditions and inheriting a high degree of ability from his father, the young master came to maturity on a journey that took him through Italy, Switzerland, France and finally to England, where he became one of the great artists of the High Renaissance in Europe. A true Olympian among draftsmen, he imparted some of his own majestic calm, nobility of soul and depth of feeling to every human being he painted. This portrait of a French Duchess is unusual in that it was drawn not from life, but from a marble tombstone.

HANS HOLBEIN THE YOUNGER
PORTRAIT OF JEANNE DE BOULOGNE,
DUCHESS OF BERRY

(Augsburg 1497—1543 London) · Portrait of Jeanne de Boulogne, Duchess of Berry · After the sculpture c. 1405 in Bourges Cathedral · C. 1524/25 · Black and colored chalks · 39,6 x 27,5 cm · Basle, Kupferstichkabinett

The life of the author of this sensitive portrait has only recently been investigated. We know merely that he was a pupil of the Bellini School in Venice, that he worked for two years for Lucrezia Borgia in Ferrara and that, after 1510, when he was in Milan, he became a devoted disciple of Leonardo, without having been one of that artist's pupils. The echoes of the tenderness, lyricism and fine modeling of the hair of Leonardo's female heads in his works led to other portraits in Frankfurt and Dresden being attributed to him. Notice the treatment of the cap, the hair and the face with its richly shaded modeling. This beautiful head reminds us how much this artist, who described himself sometimes as a Cremonese, sometimes as a Venetian, owes to Giovanni Bellini.

BARTOLOMMEO VENETO
HEAD AND SHOULDERS OF A YOUTH
WEARING A CAP

(Fl. c. 1502—1530 in Venice, Ferrara and Milan)
Head and Shoulders of a Youth Wearing a Cap
Chalk heightened with white · 38 x 28,6 cm
Vienna, Albertina

*This drawing is a study for a large painting that we know only in the first
preparatory stages. It stems from the year 1481 and was intended for the High
Altar in the chapel of the S. Donato a Scopeto convent in Florence. Notice the
confident mastery of the contours, the strong, expressive movement and the
brilliant balance of weight among the individual groups. This avoidance of
static symmetry, as in the "Last Supper" fresco, makes an apparently superficial sketch into one of the masterpieces of Italian High Renaissance drawing.
Like all Leonardo's works, this study displays ideals of beauty that were based
not only on an imaginative approach to form, but also on precise observation of
reality, and a wide knowledge of anatomy.*

LEONARDO DA VINCI
STUDY FOR THE ADORATION OF THE
THREE KINGS IN THE UFFIZI

(Vinci near Empoli 1452—1519 Cloux near Amboise)
Study for the Adoration of the Three Kings · 1481
Pen and bister · 28 x 21 cm · Paris, Louvre

The harmony of this composition, the depth and warmth of feeling and the perfection of the proportions delight the eye just as much as the massiveness and sincere piety of part and whole. The light and shade of the faces, the contact between the two women and the grace of the two boys are among the most beautiful achievements that Leonardo left behind him. Like so many other products of his multifarious activities, this masterpiece is unfinished. Today it is in the possession of the National Gallery who, when in financial difficulties in 1962, announced their intention of selling it by auction. An exhibition of the work in the National Gallery aroused great interest all over the world and sufficient money was collected by public subscription, with the help of the Government, to keep the drawing in Britain.

LEONARDO DA VINCI
MARY WITH THE CHILD JESUS
AND SAINT ANNE

(Vinci near Empoli 1452—1519 Cloux near Amboise)
Mary with the Child Jesus and Saint Anne
Charcoal · 139 x 101 cm · London, National Gallery

Dosso Dossi, celebrated by his friends as the "Ariosto of color," represents the art of the High Renaissance in the Villa d'Este. Although he absorbed much from Venice and Rome, he possessed definite individuality and, above all, a sure eye for scenes full of movement, as this lively sketch shows. It is a captivating genre study of contemporary mores and also has considerable artistic appeal. By skillful use of the laws of perspective, Dossi has given us a "snapshot" of life in a trattoria. The feast is just about to begin, and one musician is tuning his gamba, another his violin, while the serving-maid brings in the dishes and two youths enjoy a game of dice. By emphasizing the contrast between the standing figures at the edge and the horizontals of table and bench, the artist achieves such a feeling of compactness that the onlooker can take in the whole scene at a glance.

GIOVANNI DE LUTERO, DOSSO DOSSI
THE FEAST

(Dosso c. 1482—1552 Ferrara) · The Feast
Pen and wash · 24 x 22 cm · Florence, Uffizi

This Late Renaissance painter is alleged by Vasari to have been a pupil of Leonardo. However, the fact that he was one of the first sixteenth-century portrait-painters in the grand manner and painted superb court-style portraits is surely due more to the influence of Andrea del Sarto, in whose studio he worked when still only eighteen. It is no coincidence that Florence became a duchy in 1531 and that Alessandro de' Medici held his court there. As for himself, Pontormo has been described as a somewhat eccentric man, always writing in his diary. As early as 1520 the influence of Dürer's graphic art was noticeable in his work. He also spent some time in Rome where Michelangelo made a deep impression on him. Although Pontormo was an eclectic, he must be given his due as an artist of individual stamp, the last strict adherent of the style of the "golden age." This representative portrait is one of many that have been preserved.

JACOPO DA PONTORMO
HALF-LENGTH PORTRAIT OF A
SEATED MAN IN ARTISAN'S COSTUME

(Pontormo near Empoli 1494—1557 Florence)
Half-length Portrait of a Seated Man in Artisan's Costume
Charcoal · 38,5 x 25,5 cm · Florence, Uffizi

In the whole history of art there can hardly have been another work which has had such a forceful impact on generations of painters as the ceiling in the Sistine Chapel. It is peopled by a new race of "superman," idealized in anatomy, yet precise and powerfully expressive, who became as much a source of inspiration as the massive, sculptural and usually complex movements of the human body had been half a century before. As no other artist before him, Michelangelo demonstrated in his paintings and sculptures how to pervade the human form with meaning and make it the vehicle of an idea. In their titanic audacity, these studies for the athletic figure of the Libyan Sibyl show us how resolutely Michelangelo wrestled with every detail of the monumental work that occupied eight years of his life.

MICHELANGELO BUONARROTI
STUDIES FOR THE LIBYAN SIBYL

(Caprese/Casentino 1475—1564 Rome)
Studies for the Libyan Sibyl in the Sistine Chapel
Red chalk · 29 x 21,5 cm · New York,
Metropolitan Museum of Art

Like every other High Renaissance artist, Raphael used black chalk, charcoal, red chalk and pen in his drawings. In this leaf, a youthful pen-drawing, he was mainly concerned, as his teacher Perugino (1446—1524) would have been, with the lay-out of the composition. He wanted to make a group of Mary, the boy Jesus and his playmate John. Thus the three figures are merely outlined and the curves indicated by parallel and cross-hatching. Far more than any earlier drawings of the Florentine and Urbino Schools, this study shows a strong feeling for spatial values, which are discernible in spite of the simplicity of contours and technique. It is an excellent example of the qualities that made Raphael an acknowledged genius while still a young man.

RAPHAEL, RAFFAELLO SANTI
LA BELLE JARDINIÈRE

(Urbino 1483—1520 Rome) · La Belle Jardinière
(Study for the painting in the Louvre, 1507)
Pen and brush and brown ink
30,5 x 21 cm · Paris, Louvre

The merit of this drawing lies not in striking outlines but in the sensuality of the volumes and the modeling. It has not been signed, and was once attributed to Michelangelo. Modern scholars, however, have challenged this. They claim to recognize the hand of his pupil Sebastiano Luciani, who rose to fame under the name of Sebastiano del Piombo. Del Piombo was a Venetian and a pupil of both Bellini and Giorgioni. When he came to Rome in 1511, he started by following Raphael in a series of majestic half-length portraits like the beautiful "Roman Woman" in Berlin. After that master's early death, Sebastiano transferred his allegiance completely to the creator of the Sistine ceiling which caused such a furore in Rome on All Hallows, in the year 1512.

SEBASTIANO DEL PIOMBO
MADONNA AND CHILD
WITH SAINT JOHN

(Venice 1485—1547 Rome)
Madonna and Child with Saint John · C. 1530
Black chalk · 31,4 x 20 cm · London, British Museum

Rosso, a Florentine, was Court Painter to Francis I of France after the death of Leonardo. Beginning as a follower of Raphael's classical principles, or rather, those of Andrea del Sarto, he finally adopted Michelangelo's profusion of form. He was by origin a self-taught artist, and because of his eclecticism is usually relegated by art-historians to the Italian Mannerist School. On the other hand, his efforts to break with tradition are shown by the unusual grouping in this sketch, the almost Baroque depth of the background and the figures that seem ready to explode with vigor. Rosso, a humanistic, highly educated artist, problematic and philosophical rather than spontaneous, died as a canon in the Sainte Chapelle in Paris. His innumerable designs for stucco-work, wall decorations, costumes and tableware were copied all over Europe as the maniera francese, a fashion that finally faded out in Antwerp with the so-called "Floris-Stil."

ROSSO FIORENTINO,
GIOVANNI BATTISTA ROSSO
RECLINING NUDES

*(Florence 1494—1540 Fontainebleau) · Reclining Nudes
C. 1524 · Red chalk · 36 x 26,5 cm · Florence, Uffizi*

While the drawing was winning independent status as a work of art and a collector's piece, one of the most important artists of the late Renaissance in the sixteenth century was growing up. His finely molded brush drawings are far superior to his paintings. The over-slender figures in the manner of Michelangelo's much admired figure serpentinate, those men and women with spiraling forms that seem to twist round and round, betray the fact that he, as a so-called "Mannerist," was deliberately modeling his style on that of previous masters. In spite of this Parmigianino's drawings are technically outstanding and emanate the magic of great works of art. Hence they have always commanded high prices and the particular esteem of collectors.

FRANCESCO MAZZOLA, PARMIGIANINO
THE BATH OF DIANA AND CUPID

(Parma 1503—1540 Castelmaggiore)
Bath of Diana and Cupid · Pen and bister, heightened
with white on gray paper · 29,3 x 21 cm
Florence, Uffizi

Features of this drawing by one of Michelangelo's imitators indicate that it was intended as a design for some decorative purpose. The figure of the Goddess of Fortune, who appears on a wheel to symbolize the transitory nature of her gifts, was a common and popular allegorical theme at the time. Bronzino, one of the leaders of the Medici Academy that had been founded in Florence in 1561, has treated the motif with such discernment and massiveness that this leaf was once attributed to Michelangelo. In fact, the execution of the nude figure and the coarse hatching do show some similarities with the work of that master. The facial type, the languishing eyes and the cool treatment of the whole make this an important representative example of the draftmanship of Italian Mannerism. Bronzino was a pupil of Pontormo, his chief achievements being in the realm of portrait-painting.

AGNOLO BRONZINO
GODDESS OF FORTUNE ON THE WHEEL

(Monticelli, near Florence 1503—1572 Florence)
Goddess of Fortune on the Wheel · Black chalk
45,5 x 29 cm · Florence, Uffizi

Beside Fra Bartolommeo, Andrea del Sarto was the leader of High Renaissance painting in Florence. He still enjoys considerable popular esteem for his admirable "Madonna del Sacco" over the entrance to the cloisters in the Church of the Santissima Annunziata in Florence. The delicate sensitivity of his portraits, which won him many disciples, gives this almost effeminate head of a boy much of its distinctive appeal. Taking Leonardo's and Michelangelo's drawings as a basis, Andrea created some of the most sought-after red chalk drawings of his time. Although he only used traditional media he often managed to achieve Leonardo's much-prized Sfumato, or smoky effect, and much of the latter's technical expertise. Andrea also resembles Raphael in his talent for clarity, tranquillity and perfection of proportions.

ANDREA D'AGNOLO DEL SARTO
HEAD OF A BOY

(Florence 1486—1530) · Head of a Boy
(Study for John the Baptist in the Galleria Pitti)
1523 · Charcoal · 27 x 20 cm · London, British Museum

Andrea del Sarto

While Michelangelo was active in Florence and Rome, Titian was introducing a new style into Venice, a style later to develop as Baroque. There are perhaps signs of the change in this drawing. The horse is no longer seen from the side or the front, as Greek sculpture and tradition would have showed it; it is leaping across from right to left through the space of the picture, extremely foreshortened. Instead of hatching, the artist has modeled the bodies of horse and rider by smudging the charcoal lines. This technique was adopted by nearly all the draftsmen of the following Mannerist period. In this brilliant sketch Titian showed some of his talent for discovering situations and movements that no one had ever thought of before. Right up to the time of Tiepolo's ceiling frescoes his work continued to inspire and delight generations of painters.

TITIAN, TIZIANO VECELLIO
LEAPING RIDER

*(Pieve di Cadore 1476/77—1576 Venice) · Leaping Rider
C. 1550 · Black and white chalk on blue paper
38,8 x 24,7 cm · Munich, Staatliche Graphische Collection*

Landscapes without religious figures were as unknown in the fifteenth century in the North as in Italy. Studies for panel-paintings have, as far as landscape is concerned, hardly ever been preserved. They were in fact usually copied from so-called pattern-books and not kept. About 1500, however, a new interest in landscape drawing awoke in the South. In fact Dürer even brought back some water-color landscapes from his first journey to Italy (1494/95). This leaf with its romantic atmosphere was created by the same hand as the Madonna of Castelfranco, and is one of the loveliest landscape drawings of the High Renaissance. Without any solid linear framework it captures through light and shade alone that delicate S f u m a t o, or smoky effect, that Leonardo is so famous for. There can be no doubt that it was sketched in the open air outside the gates of Giorgione's native city.

GIORGIONE, GIORGIO BARBARELLI
VIEW OVER CASTELFRANCO

(Castelfranco c. 1478—1510 Venice) · View over Castelfranco · Red chalk · 20 x 29 cm Rotterdam, Boymans-van Beuningen Museum

Like Titian, Paolo Caliari of Verona, his celebrated successor, was first and foremost a painter. Although this lightly sketched head is a portrait from life, it is definitely not an independent work but probably a study for some crowded canvas. For it was Veronese who decorated the Doge's palace and other Venetian buildings with enormous pictures and frescoes that glowed with color. This semi-finished work was probably bought from the master by some connoisseur at a time when the increasing importance of drawings was inducing collectors to take an interest in occasional studies. With what genius the sensitive Veronese has created this sketch is shown by the treatment of the model's hair. The curls have been indicated with such a light hand that one could almost believe that the drawing was by one of the French Impressionists.

VERONESE, PAOLO CALIARI
HEAD OF A YOUNG WOMAN

(Verona 1528—1588 Venice) · Head of a Young Woman
Black chalk, heightened with white on blue-gray paper
34,7 x 23,1 cm · Florence, Uffizi

Although Bordone, as a pupil of Titian, is usually classed among the artists of the High Renaissance, he composed this drawing round a diagonal axis, that is, he discarded their guiding principle of symmetry. Solid and firmly outlined on the left-hand side, heightened with white on the side where the light falls, the body shows a fine borderline between the toned flesh and the background hatching. As in his pictures which are full of glowing flesh, costly silks and other surface textures, Bordone here drew like a painter. Vasari's opinion that he was "the closest imitator of Titian" cannot be taken as the sole criterion of his work today, since it clearly possessed much of the vigor and movement of the coming Baroque period, and helped to interpret the generous forms of the Renaissance masters to the generations that followed.

PARIS BORDONE · FEMALE NUDE

(Treviso c. 1500—1571 Venice) · Female Nude
Chalk, heightened with white
40 x 25,6 cm · Florence, Uffizi

This vigorous and expressive nude study is by one of Titian's most vivacious pupils, and reflects the transformations that occurred in the drawing between the period of High Renaissance and Baroque. The precise outlines have disintegrated. The linear effect is subordinate to the sculptural. Since in panel-painting the main emphasis lay in color and brushwork, the artist was content to give a general impression of form in studies like this. The Baroque sense of form lies in these rough, passionate chalk lines, now strong, now delicate, and in the spatial organization. This feeling also swept through architecture, which up till then had been geometrical and rectilinear, and made every Baroque building into a structure full of rounded contours and movement.

TINTORETTO, JACOPO ROBUSTI
MALE NUDE

(Venice 1518—1594) · Male Nude · Charcoal
25,1 x 19 cm · Florence, Uffizi

It is hardly surprising that this pupil of the aging Titian should have been so fascinated by the power of Michelangelo's works in Florence and Rome, since he himself had the same temperament. This drawing is a view from above of Michelangelo's figure of "Day" in the Medici Chapel in Florence, or perhaps of a smaller maquette, now lost. It comes from the collection of Vasari who placed it upright in his "Libro" whereas it should have been mounted horizontally since it depicts a reclining figure. When El Greco went to Spain at the age of twenty-nine, he soon forgot most of the ideas he had absorbed in Rome and devoted himself more and more to a passionate mysticism. This monumental figure has little in common with the haggard, extenuated and intellectualized types of his latter years as Spanish Court Painter. It is particularly remarkable because it shows a stage in his development, the magnificent result of the meeting of two geniuses.

EL GRECO,
DOMENICOS THEOTOCOPOULOS
STUDY AFTER A FIGURE
BY MICHELANGELO

(Crete 1541—1614 Toledo) · Study after a Figure by Michelangelo · C. 1470 · Black and white chalk on blue paper · 59,8 x 34,5 cm
Munich, Staatliche Graphische Collection

The artist of this typically courtly portrait of a young princess served as valet de chambre to four kings of France, from Francis I to Charles IX. When he took over his father's position at Court after the latter's death, he enjoyed considerable honor and a yearly pension of £ 240. In return for this, however, he had to paint coats-of-arms on flags and uniforms and model the monarch's deathmasks. He was nicknamed "Jehannet" like his father. François Clouet drew the first portraits in chalk that ever appeared in French art. Following in the footsteps of the Flemish masters, Holbein the Younger, and the Italians, Bordone and Primaticcio, he learned how to use his powers of accurate observation and painstaking, almost crabbed precision of line to produce exceptionally striking portraits. Exquisite miniatures from his hand, which are now in the Schatzkammer in Vienna, and many other pictures that bear his signature show him to have been an artist of unusual sensitivity.

FRANÇOIS CLOUET
MARGUERITE DE VALOIS

(Tours c. 1522—1572 Paris) · Marguerite de Valois, daughter of Henry II, later wife of Henry of Navarre, as a child · C. 1557 ·Black and red chalk · 34 x 22 cm Paris, Bibliothèque Nationale

Elsheimer loved to draw figures that gleam from between dark shadows, patches of chiaroscuro lit from within, and clearly structured, sculpturesque landscapes flooded with sunshine. He spent the last decade of his life in Italy where he even won some influence over the native painters. Rubens took an interest in him, Poussin learned from him, Claude Lorrain owed much to him. Even Rembrandt's forerunners came under the spell of his work by way of the engravings of the Dutchman, Goudt. This drawing, which shows how the over-slender, pathetic figures of Mannerism have given way to simple, realistic forms, reminds us of Rembrandt, as do many of his cabinet pictures. Elsheimer, known by the Italians as "Adamo Tedesco," was the last representative of the painting and drawing of the late Gothic style. After his death at an early age, German art began to draw more and more on Italy and France for inspiration.

ADAM ELSHEIMER · VENUS AND CUPID

(Frankfurt 1578—1610 Rome) · Venus and Cupid
Brush and bister · 24,8 x 20,4 cm
Berlin, Kupferstichkabinett

This harvest scene is as full of rustic gusto as every one of the powerful, vigorous pictures of the oldest "Realist" of all painters of peasant life. Bruegel has gone down in history as "Farmer Bruegel," while one of his sons, Jan the Elder (1568—1625), one of Rubens' assistants, was called "Flower Bruegel" or "Velvet Bruegel." In a figure like that of the man drinking out of the enormous pitcher, and in the naming of the drawing, Bruegel's hand may have been guided by the memory of allegorical pictures of an earlier time. In the forms of the mower and gleaners, however, he achieved peasant types that could only be the outcome of exhaustive study of nature. As always in Bruegel's works, the landscape has great depth and stretches away to infinity behind the row of trees. This particularly Dutch characteristic, accentuated here by the raised horizon, was a source of inspiration for later masters right up until the advent of Rembrandt.

PIETER BRUEGEL THE ELDER · SUMMER

(Brueghel near Breda c. 1520—1569 Brussels)
Summer · 1568 · Pen and brown ink · 22 x 28,5 cm
Hamburg, Kunsthalle

In its simplicity and grace this drawing anticipates Bernini's famous marble group in the Villa Borghese. It is by an artist who was born in Germany and educated in Italy, and shows the nymph Daphne who was transformed into a laurel tree while fleeing Apollo's amorous advances. The severe linearism of this nude points to the Northern origin of Goltzius, who later founded a school of engraving in Haarlem, which had considerable influence on Dutch art. Although this figure is Mannerist in expression and pose, it has been subtly composed out of two intersecting S-curves. The homogeneity of the background makes it seem to glow. It is far better than any of the work Goltzius did after he was forty when he developed a somewhat sterile, academic style of painting. As a painter he was not sufficiently powerful to free turn-of-the-century Dutch art from the constrictions of Southern influence. That was not destined to happen until the seventeenth century and the coming of Rembrandt.

HENDRIK GOLTZIUS · DAPHNE

(Mühlbrecht near Venlo 1558—1617 Haarlem) · Daphne C. 1600 · Pen over red and black chalk · 23,9 x 12,3 cm Munich, Staatliche Graphische Collection

This sunrise might make one think one was looking at a stage-setting for Rezia's Ocean aria in Weber's "Oberon." In fact this superb, radiant seascape is the only surviving theater design by the great sculptor and architect, Bernini. This brilliant Italian was the greatest exponent of Southern Baroque art, and the creator of the imposing canopy over the High Altar under the dome of St. Peter's. He was so versatile that Pope Urban VIII, who encouraged his studies, even wanted to make a painter out of him. Although Bernini transformed the Holy City with his palaces and fountains, he had little success as a painter and today all his pictures have disappeared. Like Rubens, he was master of a studio with innumerable assistants. His creative genius and consummate technique as a sculptor in clay and marble were still being emulated in the nineteenth century.

GIOVANNI LORENZO BERNINI · SUNRISE

(Naples 1598 —1680 Rome) · Sunrise
(Design for a Theater Décor) · Pen and wash on white
paper · 29,5 x 27,3 cm · Berlin, Kupferstichkabinett

Because of his squint, this painter was nicknamed by his contemporaries "il Guercino," the squinter. This defect did not stop him from attaining the heights of fame in Bologna, Rome and Venice. He mastered the art of drawing so early that by the age of twenty-seven he had written a text-book about it. In fact, facsimile copies of Guercino's leaves were widely available in the eighteenth century. An altarpiece of his evoked Goethe's most ardent admiration for its effective chiaroscuro — so far beyond anything which was being produced by the cold, academic school of Carracci in Bologna and the realism of Caravaggio. The fresh, almost scribbled lines of this drawing give a vivid account of a momentary impression: their sensitivity and variety are combined with a delicate and economical wash to do honor to the graphic talent of Guercino.

GUERCINO,
GIOVANNI FRANCESCO BARBIERI
STUDY OF A WOMAN BATHING

(Cento near Bologna 1591—1666 Bologna)
Study of a Woman Bathing · Pen and water-color
26 x 20,9 cm · London, British Museum

Whereas Claude Gelée from Lorraine was the foremost landscape painter of the seventeenth century, Poussin represents Roman classicism in French art, a trend that dominated right up to the nineteenth century and Ingres. For Ingres, as for Poussin, Raphael was the ideal painter of the antique style. This is why Poussin loved imaginary, heroic landscapes filled with figures from Greek history and mythology. Clothed in pure, bright raiment, perfectly balanced in posture and gesture, his mortals and Gods lead an arcadian existence undisturbed by surges of emotion or dramatic events. Even a tendency toward Baroque asymmetry, as shown in this delicately accentuated, monotone wash drawing, is an unusual find in the works of the much-debated premier peintre du roi. Poussin held this post from 1640 to 1642.

NICOLAS POUSSIN
MEDOR AND ANGELICA

(Villers near Les Andelys 1593—1665 Rome)
Medor and Angelica (Ariosto) · Pen and bister and wash
21,5 x 21,9 cm · Stockholm, National Museum

2331.   45

This attractive figure is actually an allegory of a kind that was popular right up to the nineteenth century. Taken from a series showing the five senses, it represents "Hearing," as the artist has indicated by the lute and the listening position of the head. Little is known about the artist's life. It has been established only that he worked in Nancy shortly after 1600 for fifteen years, not long after Duke Charles of Lorraine had founded a "new city" there. This study which has been dashed off with such ease is very unusual for the time. The grace and delicacy with which the Frenchman makes his red chalk scurry across the page are almost rococo, an impression which is strengthened by the fact that it has been drawn almost entirely in light and heavy strokes without stumping.

JACQUES BELLANGE · HEARING

(Fl. c. 1602—1617 Nancy)
Hearing (from a series, the "Five Senses")
Red chalk · 27 x 19,6 cm · Berlin, Kupferstichkabinett

The attraction of this study by the famous Baroque landscape painter, Claude Lorrain, lies not only in its beauty, but in its liberal conception, clear disposition of planes and convincing draftsmanship. By means of strong contrasts in the lighting, he has transformed this tree, which first captured his eye with its luxuriant color, into a monotone drawing of considerable impact. The path that winds away behind the figure in the foreground and the brightly lighted meadow complete the three-dimensional effect of the composition. It is a striking example of the way in which landscape artists achieved their effects with the simplest media, and is the French equivalent of the splendid landscapes of Rembrandt and Ruisdael which were to be painted only a few years later.

CLAUDE LORRAIN, CLAUDE GELÉE
LANDSCAPE WITH TREE AND FIGURE

*(Chamagne 1600—1682) · Landscape with Tree and Figure
Pen and bister and wash · 28,5 x 21 cm
Vienna, Albertina*

This pupil of Rubens is known chiefly for his religious paintings and his magnificent portraits. He is famous throughout the world as the founder of the English School of portrait-painting. Before this he worked in Genoa, Rome, Paris and Antwerp as an altar-painter. Thus it is all the more surprising to meet him, in this masterful study, as a landscape artist. Here he has used relaxed, almost Impressionist brush strokes to impart a magical rhythm, vitality and ambiance to a simple motif. Every tree could stand alone, but the clearing as a whole is so integrated in composition that it can be taken in at a glance. Although Van Dyck could not equal the power or vigor of his master Rubens, he did surpass him in delicacy of feeling and often in technical sensitivity. This sketch is an unusual departure for Van Dyck, and much of its appeal is due to the fact that he interpreted it with the eye of a painter rather than that of a draftsman.

ANTHONY VAN DYCK
WOODLAND SCENE

*(Antwerp 1599—1641 Blackfriars) · Woodland Scene
Water-color and gouache on blue paper · 17,8 x 25,7 cm
New York, Pierpont Morgan Library*

A. Vandyck.

The most striking clues to the period of this lavishly Baroque composition are the Mannerist forms, the arrangement of the elements and the exalted emotion of the figures' gestures and mime. The harp-playing angel, the figure in the foreground on the left and, chiefly, the ecstatic Christ and John the Baptist are all repetitions of forms that occurred frequently after the time of Michelangelo and his successors. For Michelangelo, however, every theme involving movement was a discovery, since it gave him new ways of expressing his ebullient nature. In the case of this Dutch pupil of Goltzius, on the other hand, the representation of the human form had become a technical end in itself. As a tomb-engraver he did magnificent work. Muller has approached the theme of the Baptism of Christ with a less inward eye than the Florentine and late Gothic masters would have done, because they saw it as an intimate experience.

JAN MULLER · BAPTISM OF CHRIST

(Amsterdam 1571—1628) · Baptism of Christ
Pen and india ink and wash heightened with white
29,6 x 20,8 cm · Munich, Staatliche Graphische Collection

This portrait study which is so full of tenderness and feminine grace has been drawn with a gamut of light effects that stretches from the finest cobweb-line to the deepest shadow. It proves that when he was drawing, Rubens perceived as a painter and managed to give an effect of color that only the greatest masters of drawing have achieved. There are distinct echoes of Rubens' Italian years in the beautiful pose of the young woman's hands and the way she has turned her face away from the light. In spite of his solid outlines, the artist has attained a sculpturesque quality. This is the result of his use of the finest of hatching techniques, intensified in the model's hair and sleeves to an entanglement of light, delicate lines. Deliberate virtuosity and brilliant improvisation combine to make this sketch a work of consummate draftsmanship.

PETER PAUL RUBENS
YOUNG WOMAN WITH CROSSED HANDS

(Siegen 1577—1640 Antwerp) Young Woman with Crossed Hands (probably a study for one of the saints in the Ildefonso Altar in Vienna) · C. 1630 Red, black and white chalk ·47,3 x 35,4 cm Rotterdam, Boymans-van Beuningen Museum

Like many other of Rubens' works, this equestrian portrait is unrealistic. Far removed from actuality, horse and rider incorporate the idea of material strength and the spirit of noble leadership. Representing the idealized figure of a brave commander in the Baroque period, the duke rides diagonally toward the onlooker, self-confident, indeed almost menacing. His mount, a war horse in the true sense of the word, appears to quiver at the nostrils in its eagerness for battle. However much the virtuosity of treatment in the details of armor, accouterments, mane or tail may distract the eye, dominating lines of force always guide it back from every side of the page to the conceptual center of the picture, the stern gaze of the rider. Although it is only a study, this drawing shows the figurative genius of a hand that could depict anything visible in heaven or on earth; it also shows how Rubens could wring every possible atom of expression from pen, brush and chalk.

PETER PAUL RUBENS
STUDY FOR THE PORTRAIT
OF THE DUKE OF LERMA

(Siegen 1577—1640 Antwerp) · Study for the Portrait of the Duke of Lerma · C. 1603 · Pen over black chalk and wash · 30 x 21,5 cm · Paris, Louvre

A young woman is carrying her crying child downstairs. It is Saskia, Rembrandt's beautiful wife, with Titus, then about two years old. Saskia died a few years later after only eight years of a very happy marriage. How sensitively Rembrandt captured this fleeting domestic moment. With what, almost sculpturesque, skill he has used curving pen-strokes and broad strips of wash to give light and relief to the dress and the background. What heights of perception and execution there are in the maternal tilt of the head, the child's arm anxiously clutching the mother, the child's legs, his curly hair, and the skirt that flutters behind the woman's left foot. In spite of their realistic content, every one of Rembrandt's drawings reveals his depth of soul and sovereign genius. Intoxicated as he was with beauty, he transformed every theme from human life into a masterpiece of universal truth.

REMBRANDT, HARMENSZ VAN RIJN
MOTHER AND CHILD

(Leyden 1606—1669 Amsterdam) · Mother and Child
C. 1636 · Pen and brown wash · 18,7 x 13,3 cm
New York, Pierpont Morgan Library

Rembrandt left over a thousand drawings. This is one of the most striking of them all and an audacious expression of his genius. Rembrandt was always completely objective. Here he has captured a passing physical movement with the utmost realism. The spontaneous way in which he has highlighted the body and given it firm solidarity achieves the maximum effect with the simplest of media. Though lacking the precision of an unbroken outline, the expressive, vigorous strokes and the delicate suggestions of light and shade give this accidental pose an almost sculptural appearance. The girl herself is Hendrickje Stoffels, Rembrandt's mistress during the latter part of his life. If only in the oblique Baroque pose, the choice of a back view and the depth of feeling, this study shows the hand of a genius. The gesture of the left arm and the facial expression also give us an unusual glimpse of Rembrandt's sense of humor.

REMBRANDT, HARMENSZ VAN RIJN
SEATED FEMALE NUDE FROM THE BACK

(Leyden 1606—1669 Amsterdam) · Seated Female Nude from the Back · C. 1661 · Pen and wash on brownish paper 22,4 x 18,5 cm · Munich, Staatliche Graphische Collection

5117.

In the seventeenth century, when flower-painting had been freed from the purely religious associations it still had in the works of Bruegel, a school of experts in the art gradually developed in Amsterdam. Their conscientious observation and almost photographic fidelity to nature enabled them to achieve flower-pieces of the highest perfection. Justus van Huysum (1659—1716) and particularly his son Jan, whose signature is on this colored charcoal drawing, had a style of their own, and belong among the greatest of these Dutch draftsmen and painters. Jan, who sometimes earned over 1000 guilders for a picture, did not merely imitate Nature with pictures of neat bouquets. He liked his paintings to be ablaze with movement, and the way in which he gives the onlooker a glimpse of a lighter background helps to imbue the rhythmical lines of his canvas with tempestuous life. His flowers are as expressive as the human face. Far from being merely pleasing and ornamental, they incorporate the essence of a work of art; they reveal the soul and spirit of the man who created them.

JAN VAN HUYSUM · PLANT STUDY

(Amsterdam 1682—1749) · Plant Study · 1730
Water-color over oil and charcoal · 47,5 x 35,6 cm
Paris, Louvre

If it were not well known that pastel colors were available in Dürer's day, and that they were apparently invented by a German called Thiele in Erfurt in the late Middle Ages, we would have to credit the Venetian artist, Rosalba Carriera, with the discovery of the pastel portrait. In fact, the advanced state of French pastel drawing, even that of the greatest master, Maurice Quentin de Latour (1704—1788), is due to her superb skill with the pencil. Her exhibition in Paris from 1719 to 1720 was a sensational success; she was celebrated in every court and academy as the greatest of artists, and received countless commissions. Apart from her lifelike portraits Carriera also painted miniatures that are costly collector's pieces today. This enchanting head of a girl was drawn in pale, delicate colors and has all the grace of a rococo putto. It comes from Gatschina Castle, near Leningrad, the former home of the Czar, and is now in the Hermitage. The leaf is signed on the back by the artist herself.

ROSALBA CARRIERA · HEAD OF A CHILD

(Venice 1675—1757) · Head of a Child
Pastels on light gray paper · 34 x 28 cm
Leningrad, Hermitage

Tiepolo was one of the last of the Venetian masters. As in his sweeping ceiling frescoes, the merit of this study lies in his method of fusing a wealth of detail in one comprehensive form. Whereas he often peopled the wide, empty spaces of his celestial ceilings with solitary, hovering figures, here he gave a drawing of a human back so much life that it seems like an ever-changing landscape. Tiepolo's graphic technique is magnificent. By differentiating between the thickness of stroke on the left and right shoulders and by accentuating various muscles with hatching and smudging, as well as using white highlights, the artist has given us an impression of brilliant illumination. This makes all the sculptural details merge into one massive, harmonious form.

GIOVANNI BATTISTA TIEPOLO
MALE NUDE FROM THE BACK

(Venice 1696—1770 Madrid) · Male Nude from the Back
C. 1740—1750 · Red chalk heightened with white on
blue paper · 35 x 27 cm
Stuttgart, Staatliche Graphische Collection

Canal was the son and assistant of a scene-painter. Both he and his nephew Bernardo Belotto (1720—1780), who later worked in Dresden and Vienna and died in Warsaw, have always been known by the name of "Canaletto." Antonio's most beautiful townscapes and etchings are now in England, because he worked there for some time. Although he used a camera obscura, a device for insuring accuracy in sketches, Canaletto had a real feeling for the artistic harmony that exists between buildings and figures. Even in this pen-drawing he has managed to recapture the sun-soaked atmosphere of the famous city on the Adriatic by using an almost pointilliste technique. The eye passes over the front that was built between 1423 and 1438 for the Piazetta, over St. Mark's Column, and then comes to rest on the island opposite. Above, the vault of the sky shimmers. Canaletto's contemporaries never appreciated the technical accuracy of this view, but its objectivity certainly appeals to our tastes today.

CANALETTO, ANTONIO CANAL
DOGE'S PALACE IN VENICE
OVERLOOKING S. GIORGIO MAGGIORE

(Venice 1698—1768) · Doge's Palace Overlooking
S. Giorgio Maggiore · Pen and brown ink · 27 x 18,8 cm
Windsor, Royal Library

In this portrait study in true Baroque style the simple story of the Annunciation as told by Saint Luke has been transformed into purest melodrama. The Mother of God poses coyly in front of a fragmentary column without showing a trace of inner emotion. The messenger from Heaven swoops down to her out of a cloud, accompanied by the Holy Ghost in the form of a dove. From the accentuation of the compositional diagonal, the putto dancing in front of the cloud, the passionate nobility of the poses and gestures, and the way in which broad brush strokes emphasize the color values, we can tell that this drawing is a study for an altar-painting. The late Venetian style is obvious in the painter's relaxed sense of space, and the drawing is full of the vigorous movement which gave him his strongest creative impulse.

ANTONIO GUARDI · THE ANNUNCIATION

(Venice 1698—1760) · The Annunciation
Pen and brush and brown ink over chalk · 39,5 x 28,6 cm
Munich, Staatliche Graphische Collection

After five hundred years of unbroken tradition, the Venetian school knew its last famous painter in Francesco Guardi. He used more relaxed brush strokes than his predecessor, Canaletto, but his treatment of detail was more precise. According to contemporary documents, Guardi stayed in Venice all his life. He started his career as a church painter but, after the death of his brother Gianantonio, devoted himself mostly to landscapes. His work was superior to that of the more prosaic Canaletto both in invention and spontaneity. This explains why he brought out the pictorial qualities so well in Longhena's magnificent church, the "colossal marble temple" as Goethe called it. In fact Guardi almost anticipated Monet or Renoir with some of his effects. In this drawing he paid little attention to the water and the sky, preferring to obtain his distance and depth effects with aerial perspective and shading on the buildings. Guardi was a true representative of a local school that owed much of its fame and glory to a brilliant use of color.

FRANCESCO GUARDI
SANTA MARIA DELLA SALUTE AND THE
ABBEY OF S. GREGORIO

(Venice 1712—1793) · Santa Maria Della Salute and the Abbey of S. Gregorio · C. 1765 · Black chalk and bister wash · 24,2 x 28,3 cm · Rotterdam, Boymans-van Beuningen Museum

The creator of this rococo drawing began his career in Venice, later working in Bologna, Padua and Treviso. Though fourteen years younger, the great Tiepolo assisted him in one of his later works, the "Glorification of S. Domenicus" in SS. Giovanni and Paolo in Venice, and may even have been one of Piazetta's pupils. In the somewhat self-satisfied pose and the manner in which the girl is glancing over her shoulder, this Venetian proved himself a true son of his age. At that time portrait models were almost always shown wearing a look of unconcealed vanity. The fine modeling of the face, however, makes this drawing important in its own right. It transcends the limits of a mere study and should be considered among finished works of art.

GIOVANNI BATTISTA PIAZETTA
HEAD OF A GIRL

(Pietrarossa near Treviso 1682—1754 Venice)
Head of a Girl, "El Bocolo" · Charcoal and chalk
37 x 27 cm · Venice, Accademia

This shepherd by Watteau's fellow pupil is posing with all the elegance of one of the Roi Soleil's courtiers — just as Versailles society preferred its shepherds half a century before the Revolution. We would be more likely to credit this rustic pastor with a talent for amorous dalliance than with a knowledge of the grasses and herbs that would benefit his beasts. In fact, he would fit nicely into one of the romantic comedies that were fashionable at the time. Lancret has outlined, hatched and modeled his subject directly from life without making a single correction — proof enough of the high standards of draftsmanship prevailing among the pupils of Claude Gillet. Like his more famous friend, the most brilliant of all the painters surrounding Louis XIV, Lancret was a staunch supporter of idealized genre-painting. Not before another generation had passed was it to be supplanted by the Realist-Bourgeois school of painting that foreshadowed the coming social Revolution. Again like Watteau, the creator of this study represented the age of Rococo and its frivolity. At the same time, however, he was a true son of the nation which, as Taine said, "taught all Europe the art of saluting, smiling and chatting."

NICOLAS LANCRET · SHEPHERD RESTING

(Paris 1690—1754) · Shepherd Resting · Red chalk
20,6 x 15,7 cm · Vienna, Albertina

This painter, who was born in Venice, was originally an architect. When twenty years old he traveled to Rome but was unable to obtain any commissions. Eventually he began to draw the buildings of the Eternal City, big ruins and bridges and also the hellenistic temples in Sicily. He soon became a specialist in this kind of large-scale landscape. In his best etchings and engravings we find figures that he had jotted down in the street and then cut out, so that he could fit them into his imaginative, twilight architecture according to the strictest rules of composition. His son Francesco helped him with many of these works. This view of a prison, with its distinctly operatic air, has been tossed off with masterly improvisation, and could well have been designed as a stage-setting for one of the horror operas that were fashionable in Venice a few years later. In fact, both Piranesis were scene-painters. The drawing reproduced here comes from Piranesi's series "Carceri," which includes a large number of similar prison interiors.

GIOVANNI BATTISTA PIRANESI
INTERIOR OF A PRISON

(Mogliano near Venice 1720—1778 Rome)
Interior of a Prison · C. 1744—1745
Pen and brown ink and wash over black chalk
25,6 x 18,9 cm · Hamburg, Kunsthalle

A girl with all the charm of youth, captured in a fleeting pose with the utmost spontaneity, tossed on to the paper with light pencil strokes, flooded in light with a few touches of white paint! Was she a lady's maid, a parlor-maid or a kitchen-maid in the servants' quarters of some hunting-lodge? Was she a peasant-girl at the edge of a field or a fishwife in the market? Any other painter of that period of gallantry would have visualized her as provocative and coquettish, or would have placed her in the sociological scale by some literary allusion. Watteau, however, an ironic genius amidst that frivolous company, contented himself with showing her natural human appeal, and framed her in the spirited polyphony of a lilting line. We hardly know what we should admire most — the triangular shape of the whole composition, the lively expression on the face, or the sweep of the lines. Any one of these alone would make this drawing a masterpiece of French graphic art.

JEAN-ANTOINE WATTEAU
SEATED WOMAN

(Valenciennes 1684—1721 Nogent-sur-Marne)
Seated Woman · Red, black and white chalk
25,4 x 17,1 cm · New York, Pierpont Morgan Library

More than any other study by the leading French master of the eighteenth century, this nude reminds us of the many works by the School of Rubens that Watteau must have seen in the churches of his native city. In Paris, also, he had every opportunity of studying the twenty-one colossal scenes from the life of the Virgin Mary which were commissioned by Maria de' Medici and Henry IV for the Louvre and executed by Rubens and his pupils. This study of an extremely unusual arm movement, treated with such sensitivity, shows us how much French art had derived from Flemish-Walloon painting. Nevertheless, it is also full of an elegance that is truly French — an elegance that reflects the transition from the luxuriance of Baroque to the refined sensuality of rococo. It is also unusual to find a nude among Watteau's works, since his talent lay so much more in clothed figures that he set the dress fashions of the day.

JEAN-ANTOINE WATTEAU · FEMALE NUDE

(Valenciennes 1684—1721 Nogent-sur-Marne)
Female Nude · Red and black chalk · 28,3 x 23,2 cm
Paris, Louvre

Boucher, the "painter of the Graces," was unlike later artists in that he always chose literary or mythological titles for his drawings. This beautiful woman was drawn in 1752 and reminds us of the great painters he took for an example, Giorgione, Titian and Veronese. He did not, however, always attain their nobility of style or their compositional harmony. For Boucher was a rococo artist, and he dragged the Gods and Goddesses of his greater predecessors down to the level of the salons of his day. His accentuation of the provocative, for instance, is essentially French and typical of the atmosphere of eighteenth-century Parisian society life. This is probably why Boucher, with his decorative rather than inspired painting, fell into a style that was often superficial and full of clichés. His versatility as a decorator, designer and director of the Royal Gobelin works brought him more success at the time than fame afterward. While he painted nearly all his nudes from memory, his drawings were almost certainly drawn from life. They are among some of the best of his works.

FRANÇOIS BOUCHER
RECLINING FEMALE NUDE
FROM THE BACK

*(Paris 1703—1770) · Reclining Female Nude from the Back · Red and black chalk heightened with white and some pink · 14,9 x 29,8 cm
Cologne, Wallraf-Richartz-Museum*

Though forgotten in his old age, which coincided with a period of classical historical painting, Fragonard returned to fame after his death. He was the most important of Boucher's pupils, and is chiefly known for his realistic genre-paintings. His style, like that of his master, was admirably suited to the prevailing taste for lightweight pictures and a courtly way of life. Fragonard came from Grasse, near Nice, and spent several years in Rome. However frivolous his "Woman Bathing" and his "Shepherd Scenes" may seem to us today, we must admit that this is a masterly landscape drawing. It was sketched in Italy, where he had been most influenced by Tiepolo. By the use of large forms and a wealth of detail, the artist captured the full shimmering heat of a Southern summer's day and, at the same time, found the perfect way of treating the foreground, middle ground and background.

JEAN-HONORÉ FRAGONARD
AVENUE OF POPLARS IN THE GARDENS
OF THE VILLA D'ESTE IN TIVOLI

*(Grasse 1732—1806 Paris) ·Avenue of Poplars
in the Gardens of the Villa d'Este in Tivoli · C. 1760
Red chalk and bister · 46,6 x 34,2 cm · Vienna, Albertina*

Saint-Aubin, an appealing but minor master, achieved a wonderful feeling of sunshine in this "reporter's eye view" of a garden-party. It combines the essence of both landscape and figure-drawing. Even though the tree-tops with their varied and lively shading may lack the sculpturesque conviction of a Watteau or a Fragonard, the depth and delicate treatment of the space above the dancers gives ample proof of the skill Saint-Aubin had learned from his master, Boucher. In the most finely graduated steps, the artist constructed a third of his composition entirely out of figures. The result is the illusion of a wide-open space filled with music and merrymaking, which contrasts strongly with the lantern-garlands between the trees and the strong tones of the foreground. An observant eye and a practiced hand have made this study of eighteenth-century society life into a delightful historical document.

AUGUSTIN DE SAINT-AUBIN
THE BALL NEAR GRIEL IN SAINT-CLOUD

(Paris 1736—1807) · The Ball near Griel in Saint-Cloud
1759 · Pen and wash in Chinese ink and sepia
21,6 x 17 cm · Paris, Louvre

The creator of this graceful head of a girl studied in Lyon before settling in Paris. The fame he enjoyed among his contemporaries was mainly due to his genre-paintings and his studies of the everyday life of the times. His work was strongly influenced by the bourgeois theater of the day, and therefore has a rather critical flavor, appealing little to our modern taste because of its sentimental undertones. Greuze's many rather sugary portraits were painted to sell well. On the other hand, Greuze achieved effects, as in this study, in which it is not only the model's charm that bewitches. Here he displays a graphic talent far superior to the craftsmanship of his painting. Thus his study can rightfully claim its place as a work of art of lasting value. That the artist has placed the head in an oblique position is not only due to coincidence; it is a last faint echo of the Baroque taste for diagonal compositions.

JEAN-BAPTISTE GREUZE
STUDY OF THE HEAD OF A GIRL

(Toumus 1725—1805 Paris)
Study of the Head of a Girl
Pastels on a red chalk ground · 34 x 26 cm
Vienna, Albertina

No longer playful and coquettish as was the previous generation, Prud'hon, a contemporary of Mozart, was inspired by the spirit of classicism. Here he has drawn an admirable portrait of his favorite model, Marguerite. Grave, solemn, almost exalted, this nude reminds us of an antique marble statue with its finely differentiated hatching that is always vertical even in the deepest shadows, and the concise outlines of the body. The figure is illuminated by bright light from above. Prud'hon, who was born in Cluny and who studied in Rome, found it difficult to compete with the historical painter David, who was politically active during the Revolution and under Napoleon, and who founded French classicism. Although he is sometimes underestimated, Prud'hon's mythological paintings, which won him the title of the "French Correggio" and a following even among the Romantic school, and above all his portrait of the Empress Josephine, have insured him a permanent place in the history of French art.

PIERRE-PAUL PRUD'HON
STUDY OF A FEMALE NUDE

(Cluny 1758—1823 Paris) · Study of a Female Nude (Marguerite) · C. 1814 · Black and white chalk on blue-gray paper · 28 x 22 cm · Formerly in the Laporte Collection, Philadelphia, Pa.
Collection of Henry P. McIlhenny

William Hogarth was the great forerunner of such painters as Wilson, Reynolds, Gainsborough and Romney. With his appearance, English art freed itself from the influence of Italian and Dutch academism and rose suddenly to independent heights of greatness. This brilliant realist grasped at the very heart of life itself. He perceived it with an élan that borders on caricature, and became a moral painter of the first rank. With brush and etching or engraving chisel, he told a gripping story and, like Molière, lashed out at the vices and follies of mankind. His work was truly original, though he had his great followers in Goya and Daumier. Thanks to a power of observation that was greedy for every detail, Hogarth did not shun even the lowest of evil haunts. Far from embodying the idealistic reflections expressed in his book "Analysis of Beauty" (1753) which made many concessions to popular taste, he became the most acute critic of the age. In milieu sketches like this scene from a smoke-hazy, alcohol-blurred quayside tavern, Hogarth showed himself to be the graphic counterpart to the author of the "Beggar's Opera."

WILLIAM HOGARTH · TAVERN SCENE

(London 1697—1764 Chiswick) · Tavern Scene
Pen and water-color · 21,5 x 28,5 cm
London, British Museum

A few brief charcoal lines on a tinted ground, heightened with a faint veil of white chalk — this completely unacademic improvisation by the first President of the Royal Academy might almost be modern in its economy of line. It is even more of a surprise when we realize that Reynolds spent three years in Rome during which he modeled his style on that of Titian and Correggio. As Royal Court Painter, it was some time before he could conceive of a portrait without some mythological draperies. Unlike his more worldly colleague, Gainsborough, Reynolds had to wait until he was a mature man before he could free himself from these literary or intellectual millstones. Once he had rid himself of them, however, he began to paint portraits in superb color, particularly many fresh and graceful portraits of children. The drawing reproduced here, which may be either an embryo Court portrait or a private sketch, shows us Reynolds from the side which appeals most to us today; it was drawn at a time when British art was at its peak.

SIR JOSHUA REYNOLDS
PORTRAIT OF A CHILD

(Plympton 1723—1792 London) · Portrait of a Child
Charcoal and white chalk on blue paper · 29 x 20,5 cm
London, British Museum

When the Royal Academy was founded under Sir Joshua Reynolds in 1768, Gainsborough was at the zenith of his career as a fashionable society painter. In fact he painted King George III and his family no fewer than eight times. Ignorant of classical art, primarily self-taught and only occasionally influenced by Dutch or Spanish art, Gainsborough, with his light, pleasing and elegant portraits, reminds us often of Watteau. With a fluidity of exposition and emphasis on color-harmonies, as in this drawing, the creator of the famous "Blue Boy" left it to the onlooker to discover the subtle chromatic effects in his paintings. It is characteristic of this artist that he used the narrow edge of his pastels to draw the lines, then turned over to the broad edge for the planes, rather than using the highly developed, delicate smudge technique that was current in France at the time.

THOMAS GAINSBOROUGH
PORTRAIT OF GEORGIANA,
DUCHESS OF DEVONSHIRE

(Sudbury 1727—1788 London)
Portrait of Georgiana, Duchess of Devonshire
(1757—1806) · Black and white chalk · 48,8 x 30,6 cm
New York, Pierpont Morgan Library

This drawing is by the little-known but extremely individual Swiss artist Füssli, who won great renown in London. His superb drawing of a well-built girl at her toilet reveals a knowledge of antique sculpture and considerable experience of Southern art. The en face pose and the composition — we only have to look at the accentuated verticals and diagonals — anticipate much of the work of French Classicists like David or Prud'hon. Füssli, who called himself "Fuseli" in England, later became one of the most original of the early Romantics and we might almost consider him as a forerunner of Delacroix. With his weird, romantic faces and, above all, his apparitions that might have come out of "The Tempest" he made a great impression on his friend, William Blake (1757—1827). Although Füssli was an important link in the chain that led to the Surrealists, this classical leaf shows that he was also a disciple of those classical masters who paid homage to the beauty of the female form without being burdened by intellectual combat with the supernatural.

JOHANN HEINRICH FÜSSLI (FUSELI)
NUDE

(Zurich 1741—1825 London) · Nude
Water-color on gray-green paper · 18,5 x 15 cm
London, British Museum

The "Michelangelo of landscape-painting" was what Ruskin called the creator of this sea scene, and though the claim may seem somewhat exaggerated today, we must still admit that Turner's landscapes rank high above the paintings of any of his European contemporaries. They were even an occasional source of inspiration for the French Impressionists. For Turner was one of the few historical painters whose works still grip and move us today. Inspired by Claude Lorrain, he became a painter of light of the highest order. In his marine paintings, Turner gave life at sea a dramatic content like no other painter before him. Sometimes realistic and glowing, sometimes visionary and imaginative, sometimes dreaming and voluptuous, Turner's pictures are always technically individual and outstanding. His awareness of life and the spirit of the times is shown by the fact that he was already including railways and steamships in his paintings, while French and German artists were still thinking in terms of idealism and romanticism.

WILLIAM TURNER · SAILING SHIPS

(London 1775—1851 Chelsea) · Sailing Ships
21,5 x 28,3 cm · Water-color · London, British Museum

Ingres' art depends far more than any other artist of the previous century on the expressive power of the line. His clearly constructed Empire portraits are among some of the most beautiful pictures in the Louvre in Paris. In consequence Ingres was hailed by many as the "Raphael of the nineteenth century." Owing to his undisputed position of authority in the eighteen-thirties, Ingres reigned as a kind of High Priest of orthodox art in Paris for several decades. This graphically excellent portrait of the Italian who held all his contemporaries spellbound and who founded the modern school of violin-playing, should remind us that Ingres himself was no mean violinist. Indeed, the French expression "violon d'Ingres" is the equivalent of our word "hobby," and is derived from the painter's passion for the instrument. As a historical document this admirable drawing is as vivid as it is well-executed.

JEAN-AUGUSTE-DOMINIQUE INGRES
PORTRAIT OF PAGANINI

*(Montauban 1780—1867 Paris) · Portrait of Paganini
Rome 1819 · Pencil · 29,5 x 21,5 cm · Paris, Louvre*

Goya has been called the most Spanish of all Spanish painters. This is even truer of his oil or graphic portraits than of his late Baroque church paintings or his many genre fantasies and satires. Inexorable, sometimes even prosaic, objectivity, which he borrowed from Rembrandt, is the keynote of this portrait sketch. It is typical of the work of Goya, the brilliant illustrator, whose influence was still strong many years after his death. Throughout his life Goya was tormented by the demon of his genius and his inner conflicts; he was a true spiritual fellow-countryman of Cervantes. Although he was Director of an Academy and Court Painter to several Kings, for some reason not yet fully explained he had to spend his last years in exile. In spite of the rigorousness, almost sharpness of the lines, and in spite of the coincidental nature of the material, this brush-drawing has an almost classical harmony and tranquillity. Although Goya generally used a temperamental, free graphic technique that made him a revered ancestor of the Impressionists, this leaf gives us an instance of a style that is strictly linear. Goya, who was chiefly influenced by Velásquez in his early years, also came into contact with the tendencies of French classicism, and was still an important figure of that period in extreme old age.

FRANCISCO DE GOYA
PORTRAIT OF DON FRANCISCO DE BORJA

(Fuentetodos 1746—1828 Bordeaux)
Portrait of Don Francisco de Borja, Tenth Duke of Osuna
(Study for the Portrait in the Musée Bonnat, Bayonne)
Pen and brush and bister · 25 x 18,3 cm · Madrid, Prado

Idea p.ᵃ el retrato qe pinto Goya del Duque de
Osuna y existe en el Palacio del act.ᵒ Duque su bis...

Schadow was the "Director of all Sculpture" and master of the Court Sculpture Studies in Berlin. His particular form of painstaking accuracy and strict faithfulness to nature was criticized even at the time. The objections raised, however, were not the same as we should voice today. Goethe, for example, spoke out against this exaggeratedly antique naturalism in "Die Propyläen," and demanded a more idealistic approach to the model. Even though this portrait of a Berlin actress may seem over-idealized to us today, its fundamentally academic technique does seem to display the *grace and dignity*, in Schiller's sense of the words, that all artists were searching for during the time of the Napoleonic Wars. Sculptor of the Quadriga on the Brandenburg Gate, Schadow has set up a lasting memorial with this portrait of a beautiful woman of the time. It is far superior to many contemporary paintings. Without a moment's hesitation, he gave his model a daringly chic hair-style that has a distinct air of Paris about it, although such revolutionary insinuations were regarded as highly suspicious in the Royal Prussian Court at the time.

GOTTFRIED SCHADOW
PORTRAIT OF THE ACTRESS UNGER

(Berlin 1764—1850) · Portrait of the Actress Unger
Black and colored chalk · 37,5 x 26,5 cm
Berlin, Akademie der Künste

It was the idea of decorating the museum of antique sculpture with frescoes that first led King Ludwig of Bavaria to summon the Rhineland artist Cornelius to Munich in 1820. Up till then Cornelius had been working in Frankfurt and as Director of an Academy in Düsseldorf, his main works being drawings of "Faust" and the "Nibelungs" in the Romantic Late-Gothic spirit. While in Rome, as leader of a Neo-Gothic group of artists, who called themselves in monastic nostalgia Pre-Raphaelites and Nazarenes, Cornelius' lofty artistic ethos also had a considerable influence on painters like Friedrich Overbeck, Philipp Veit and Julius Schnorr von Carolsfeld. Even though his colossal picture, "The Last Judgment," above the altar in the Ludwigskirche in Munich (1836—1840), is hardly considered worth a glance today, and seems cold and academic, Cornelius was still the most distinctive personality in the art world of the first half of the century. In this design he followed the classical leanings of the king and sought inspiration from the sculptures on the Parthenon, as we can tell from the bodies of the horses and the deep frieze beneath them.

PETER CORNELIUS · DESIGN FOR A
CEILING PAINTING IN THE GLYPTOTHEK
IN MUNICH

(Düsseldorf 1783—1867 Berlin)
Design for a Ceiling Painting in the Glyptothek
in Munich · Pencil and pen and water-color and body-color
20,5 x 39,9 cm · Munich, Städtische Galerie

Unaffected by the Impressionists' struggle for naturalism, yet imposing and powerful in his own province, Hans von Marées had a very personal form of expression. In its classical peace and tranquillity, this study shows how the master was content to dispense with every realistic detail in his concern with representing the sheer essence of humanity. His figures and animals are grouped in complete harmony with their surroundings; they are shapes from another idealistic world, who neither act nor suffer, but just are. Deeper, warmer and more poetic than his other colleagues with classical leanings, von Marées achieved his greatest ambitions under the influence of the southern sun. In Italy, where he came in contact with the art-lover and theorist, Konrad Fiedler, and Adolf Hildebrand, the sculptor, he produced his best work. This includes the impressive frescoes in Naples and the incomparable Munich paintings. They stand alone amidst the art of nineteenth-century Germany.

HANS VON MARÉES
CHARIOT AND PAIR AND GROUP
OF WOMEN

(Elberfeld 1836—1887 Rome)
Chariot and Pair and Group of Women · C. 1880
Red chalk · 39 x 40,5 cm
Munich, Staatliche Graphische Collection

Among a whole host of classically minded academics of the eighteen-thirties who have been forgotten long ago, Daumier, the great satirist and judge of human nature, stands out like a mountain peak. Although few people know of him as a painter in the eighteen-fifties and -sixties, Daumier is famous for the lithographs that appeared in the newspapers "Caricature" and "Charivari," in which he anticipated the bourgeois revolutions of 1830 and 1848, and helped to give them an intellectual stimulus. At the same time, however, Daumier was preparing the way for the then modern realism of Courbet and Millet, and the Impressionists. With the large forms and Cézanne-like clarity and stringency of this drawing, he has immortalized his friend Corot, as the latter sits in the garden of his country-house, reading a book. In spite of the linear technique, Daumier's broad planes here anticipate the sun-dappled effects that Renoir was to discover some time later.

HONORÉ DAUMIER · THE PAINTER
COROT IN VILLE D'AVRAY

(Marseilles 1810—1879 Valmondois)
The Painter Corot in Ville d'Avray · C. 1854
Pen and water-color · 31,5 x 24,5 cm
New York, Metropolitan Museum of Art

In the year 1818 Aloys Senefelder, an unsuccessful actor from Bohemia, published a book which described his invention of lithograph printing late in the previous century. This method of reproduction was quickly adopted by all the French newspapers. Like Honoré Daumier, Gavarni owed the tremendous success of his caricatures in "Charivari" and "Illustration" to lithography. Gavarni was actually named Hippolyte Sulpice-Guillaume Chevalier. His pseudonym was taken from the name of the magnificent natural phenomenon near the village of Gavarnie, the "Cirque de Gavarnie," a gorge, over a mile high and a mile wide, whose largest waterfall thunders down from glacier-level 500 yards up. The artist was particularly fond of this mountainous spot, although it was rarely visited at the time. As a critic of political and social conditions in the juste milieu of Louis-Philippe, and although closer to life and less caustic than the satiric Daumier, during the Second Empire, Gavarni's witty series had just as strong an effect on his times as those of his more famous colleague. His "Masques et Visages," 1857, from which these haunting figures are taken, should be classed with the fantastic creations of the Romantic Realist art that followed Goya.

PAUL GAVARNI · MY HUSBAND!

(Paris 1804—1866 Paris) · My Husband!
Pastel heightened with white · 28,9 x 22,4 cm
Budapest, Szépmüvészeti Mùséum

Millet was the son of a Brittany peasant, and all his paintings of peasant life give a feeling of earnestness, tinged with social awareness. The same earnestness pervades this everyday scene, especially the figure of the little girl, who shows by the tilt of her head and the position of arms and legs that she is witnessing a natural occurrence. Millet, a precursor of the sterner realism of Courbet, has used soft hatching to give this somewhat banal theme almost as much solemnity as his famous "Gleaners" and the "Angelus," which is now in the Louvre. In all these genre-paintings there lurks some of the horror of the riots of July, 1830, but their nobility of feeling raises them high above the homely sentimentality of their period. This drawing, like Millet's paintings, shows how he saw the peasants objectively as peasants, not as the "countryfolk" of classical poetry. In fact, romanticism was giving way to naturalism. Already in 1833 an art critic had attacked Delacroix by saying "True art, the art of the future, will be realistic!" Seven years later Millet's first paintings had a tremendous success in the Salon.

JEAN FRANÇOIS MILLET
THE CARES OF MOTHERHOOD

(Gruchy 1814—1875 Barbizon)
The Cares of Motherhood · Chalk · 29,8 x 23 cm
Budapest, Szépmüvészeti Mùséum

Throughout Delacroix' work we see how deeply he had been affected by his childhood experiences of the brutality and cruelty of death. Following in the footsteps of the great Italians of the Renaissance and Baroque, Delacroix has imbued a well-worn theme with all the vigorous spirit of romanticism. As leader of the Romantic movement, he was not contented merely to represent extravagant grief, as we know it from such paintings as Van Dyck's sepultures. Instead he has given every figure, even the body of Christ, which is posed so as to give the maximum expressive force, the passionate ardor of his genius. The composition is as concentrated as a group of sculpture, and every individual form has an almost overwhelming intensity. This is due to the expressive technique and fiery personality of Delacroix, who dedicated so much of his life to the cause of art, and who, as Ingres' most formidable opponent, conquered the classicism that had grown sterile with a revolution of form and color.

FERDINAND VICTOR EUGÈNE DELACROIX
DESCENT FROM THE CROSS IN
SAINT-DENIS DU SAINT-SACREMENT

(Charenton-St. Mauricel 1798—1863 Paris)
Descent from the Cross in Saint-Denis du Saint-Sacrement
1841—1843 · Pen · 20,5 x 31 cm · Paris, Louvre

Manet not only introduced an entirely new approach to color, but was also the first artist to emphasize the importance of light in his pictures, as he has done here. This pen-and-ink drawing has been given solid form not by sculpturesque modeling, but by the contrast of bigger and smaller, lighter and darker surfaces, and by the use of the same sparkling dot and comma technique that lends such a shimmer to his colorful landscapes. At the same time the surface of the drawing, as a whole, differs from the work of later Impressionists in having occasional portions that are almost architectural in organization. From the skirt over the sleeve, the glove, the waist, from the parasol-stick over the hatband, face and hat-trimming this superb drawing has been built up piece by piece right up to the foliage behind the head. Because of the large repertoire of graphic techniques Manet used here, almost as many as Van Gogh was to use in his sketches, the whole leaf gleams and shines in myriad variations of form and shape. It is a masterpiece, both in the perception and in the subtle way that Manet has suggested the al fresco atmosphere of spring.

ÉDOUARD MANET · SPRING

*(Paris 1832—1883) · Spring · 1881 · Pen and india ink
31,3 x 21,2 cm · Cambridge, Mass., Fogg Museum of Art*

"In art nothing must happen by chance, not even movement," Degas once said. And he made a passionate study of what the Goncourt brothers regarded as the "monkey-tricks" of "suburbanites." Thus he never tired of taking up his pen or pencil to sketch the endless variety of gestures that could be observed in the Ballet Room of the Opéra where the young dancers were practicing. Just as Claude Monet recorded color impressions of a landscape between changes of light, so Degas captured the fleeting positions à la barre, where the girls were stretching their muscles and joints. The delicate, misty, downy-soft effects in the hair and tutus of the dancers are achievements that no other French Impressionist has equaled. Degas' pastels and oils represent the peak of the glorification of color — a peak that was unsurpassed before the great transition took place, and European art changed from the material and figurative to the immaterial and abstract.

EDGAR DEGAS · DANSEUSES

(Paris 1843—1917) · Danseuses · Pastels · 114 x 83 cm
Washington, D. C., Phillips Collection

It was not Cézanne's ambition to record fleeting impressions of light and color on his canvas like Monet, or to achieve an "optical effect of color," like Renoir. This is why he soon parted company with the other Impressionists, although, for instance, he still esteemed Pissarro very highly as a teacher. With the same fervor that characterizes Van Gogh and Gauguin, he struggled unceasingly to perfect a new kind of pictorial structure, since he soon realized that Impressionism must lead to the disintegration of form. With brush strokes that are relaxed, yet crystalline in shape, he found his own way of interpreting the sensations colorées that fascinated him in nature, reproducing them as a clearly ordered pattern without spatial reference. With this, Cézanne turned away from the century-old ideals of imitation of Nature, and became the great inspirer and instigator of twentieth-century art. In definite, broad verticals and horizontals, supported by infrequent patches of color, Cézanne has "realized" (his own word) this view of the famous mountain near Aix-en-Provence, the mountain that he loved and painted so often.

PAUL CÉZANNE · MOUNT SAINT-VICTOIRE

(Aix-en-Provence 1839—1906) · Mount Saint-Victoire
Water-color · 22,3 x 29,9 cm · Paris, Private Collection

This drawing by the master of Impressionist figure-painting is a study for "La Danse à la Campagne," a lively canvas which has its counterpart in Renoir's earlier work, "La Danse à la Ville," which is based on portraits of Mr. and Mrs. Sisley. As so often in Renoir's middle years, this study was probably inspired by a scene in the Rowing Clubs by the Seine or the suburban Paris bistros that he and his friends frequented at the time. More than any other painter, Renoir seemed to see in terms of palette, brush and the finished composition. It is characteristic of his way of sketching that he only indicated the heads and positions of the dancing couple. Everything else for him was purely a matter of color. In this study, as in the completed painting, it is chiefly the quality of timelessness that impresses us, the poetical approach that is revealed in the intensity of expression and the way the partners have abandoned themselves to the music. With this poetry the master has shown us the true depth of his personality. This drawing is also a portrait of Suzanne Valadon, a professional model and the mother of Maurice Utrillo. She later became a painter in her own right.

AUGUSTE RENOIR · COUPLE DANCING

(Limoges 1841—1919 Cagnes) · Couple Dancing
(Study for the Painting "La Danse à la Campagne" in the
Durand-Ruel Collection) · 1883 · 23,8 x 11,9 cm
Budapest, Szépmüvészeti Mùséum

Disgusted by modern civilization, Gauguin periodically fled France, going first to Martinique and in later years to the South Sea Islands which were still uncorrupted by "education." He soon felt himself to be an outcast from the naturalistic art of illusion as practiced by the Impressionists, but sadly enough no one in France would buy his pictures. Spread over the surface, in broad masses, enclosed by clear outlines, his girls and women in color and pencil give the effect of stone figures. They are never nervous or refined in interpretation, but earthbound and heavy, animal-like in their essential innocence. We sense the influence of the Japanese wood-cuts that Van Gogh had introduced him to. These studies by the brilliant recluse could have been conceived only with a painting in mind, and are proofs of the gradual development of art towards Modern Art. With the discovery of Gauguin's advances into new artistic territory, Impressionism was recognized for, as Van Gogh once wrote, "optical illusion." This now had to give way to the important realization that a work of art was anything but a repetition of some object in Nature.

PAUL GAUGUIN
WOMEN FROM MARTINIQUE

(Paris 1848—1903 Fatu-Iwa, Marquesas)
Women from Martinique · 1887 · Pastels · 48,5 x 64 cm
Paris, Private Collection

"Art is man allied with the Nature that he liberates," Van Gogh wrote to his brother Theo. The artist should always find *"the treasured pearl that has been brought to light, the human soul"* in the outside world, *"even when he is drawing tiles, granite, iron bars or the arches of a bridge."* Van Gogh, whose heart was not only moved by the dramatic but always attuned to dramatization, became one of the fathers of German Expressionism. In this powerful sketch he looked at some humble fishing-boats as no other artist had looked at them for centuries before him. At the same time he entirely deserted the earlier Impressionist techniques that he was using before the hunger for light drove him southward. With broad black and white surfaces, tense lines and a very individual dotted treatment to give the effect of the sand, Van Gogh gave this study for a famous painting a compelling rhythmical content. Its success is not just a matter of seeing, but of feeling; it is not a copy, but a symbol. Scoured sands, calm seas, four boats and some gulls hovering overhead are here almost incomparable in conception and force. They have received that *"realism full of grandeur,"* that *"heroism of reality"* that Cézanne demanded from the artist.

VINCENT VAN GOGH
STUDY FOR THE SAILING-BOATS
NEAR SAINTES-MARIES

(Groot Zundert 1853—1890 Auvers-sur-Oise)
Study for the Sailing-boats near Saintes-Maries · 1888
Brush drawing · 29,5 x 53,5 cm
Munich, Tschudi Collection

Like all the French painters after the middle of the nineteenth century, Seurat had a particular liking for themes from the theater and the circus. An artist who died all too early, he was the leader of the Pointillism movement which was struggling to re-establish a stricter sense of form. Different in every way from, say, Monet or Renoir, Seurat created the illusion of depth and light with his minute dot technique; all the dark parts are achieved by differing densities of dots, contrasted with empty spaces. The effect has been intensified by the use of a rough-grained paper. Seurat was searching for the permanent behind the momentary appearance, the "impression," as Monet called it in the title of one of his paintings. He always gave weight to this permanent element by the clear structural composition of his pictures. Although he used only the most economical of media, in this drawing Seurat managed to imbue the half-light of the stage with the magic atmosphere of the cabaret, and to fill the air with a swarm of tones. He chose a profile position for the sake of form and outline.

GEORGES SEURAT
THE COFFEE-HOUSE SINGER

*(Paris 1859—1891) · The Coffee-House Singer
C. 1887 · Chalk heightened with white · 31,5 x 24,4 cm
Laaren, Holland, Collection of V. W. Van Gogh*

The brilliant painter and draftsman of old Montmartre is most widely acclaimed for his caricatures of entertainers and dance-hall habitués. That he was also a portrait-painter is less generally known. A great variety of his portraits are hung together today in the medieval palace near the cathedrale of Albi where they attract visitors from all over the world. In this lightning sketch which sparkles with life and humor, and shows a sure grasp of graphic techniques, the French count has immortalized a chance encounter with a young woman. With the most delicate sense of form and expression he felt his way, psychologically, into his model, and sketched her features with the subtlest of lines. "You draw abominably," Bonnat once said to his eighteen-year-old pupil. It was Degas who first recognized the gifts of the rich and aristocratic young man, who, like Degas, did not have to make a living from his art and whose pictures have commanded extremely high prices since his death.

HENRI DE TOULOUSE-LAUTREC
THE ENGLISHWOMAN FROM THE "STAR"
CABARET IN LE HAVRE

(Albi 1864—1901 Château Malromé, Gironde)
The Englishwoman from the "Star" Cabaret in Le Havre
(Study for the painting) · 1899
Red chalk heightened with white · 62 x 47 cm
Albi, Musée Toulouse-Lautrec

Born in Lowell, Massachusetts, the son of a drawing teacher and military engineer, James Abbott McNeill Whistler spent part of his childhood in Russia, where his father was engaged in building railroads. After three years at the United States Military Academy at West Point, he worked briefly as a draftsman, then went to Paris in 1855 to study painting and settled in London four years later. With his famous "Portrait of the Painter's Mother," now in the Louvre, Whistler was the first American artist to win international honors at the Venice Biennial. A facile craftsman with rare understanding of his media, Whistler worked with equal ease in oil, pastel, lithography, and etching. He is today considered with Rembrandt, Claude Lorrain, Van Dyck, and Dürer as one of the greatest etchers of all time. Although nearly three hundred of his etchings are recorded, the number of his paintings and drawings is limited. The paintings, which show independence in their approach, are sensitive in color and tone, yet boldly designed and strongly influenced by the work of Japanese printmakers which was only then being introduced to Europe. This quality of bold design is also evident in his drawings, which are intimate, vivacious and slight, and often, as his pastels of the human figure, exquisite. Though done in charcoal, "Maude Reading" is broadly handled, yet, through its sureness of line and masterful control of light and shade and with deft highlight touches in white chalk, it suggests a great interest in detail.

JAMES ABBOTT McNEILL WHISTLER
MAUDE READING

(Lowell, Mass. 1834—1903 London) · Maude Reading
Charcoal and white chalk on brown paper
16,8 x 12,7 cm · Washington, D. C., Smithsonian
Institution (Freer Gallery of Art)

Winslow Homer, possibly the greatest artist of the United States in the last half of the nineteenth century, was born in Boston. Initially a freelance illustrator, he became an artist on "Harper's Weekly" in 1859 and was, in the years immediately following, one of that magazine's artist-reporters during the American Civil War. After a visit to Paris in 1866/67, he developed a confirmed interest in recording the simple values of rural life in New England, which he did with great charm, mainly in water-colors and drawings. This second period of his work closed with a visit to Tynemouth, England, in 1881/82. Thereafter he devoted himself to powerful paintings of the Maine coast and the working life of its fishermen. In his later period he also did a large number of popular water-colors of Bermuda, the Bahamas and Florida, and the Adirondack Mountains. Homer's drawings, which number in hundreds, are simply and dramatically conceived. His later ones are very broadly drawn in charcoal. This Study for "The Wreck of the Iron Crown" employs, as do most of his drawings, strong design and skillful use of light and shade to heighten its effectiveness. Here we have a counterpoint of action and areas of calm: men making fast the small boat swung from davits on a ship at sea. The simple form of the lifeboat, the arched lines of the davits, the horizontal handrail and benches, provide a stable balance to the activity of the men and the swelling angry sea in the background. The whole seems rendered with great ease and effortless economy.

WINSLOW HOMER · STUDY FOR "THE WRECK OF THE IRON CROWN"

(Boston 1836—1910 Prout's Neck, Maine)
Study for "The Wreck of the Iron Crown"
Pencil and water-color on brown paper · 34,5 x 48,4 cm
New York, Cooper Union Museum

Few other painters have revealed such an intense form of the French classical sense of clarity and order as has Matisse. In his drawings there are none of the Impressionists' soft, twilight moods. Also Matisse never recorded momentary impressions. "My line drawings are the direct and purest interpretation of my feelings," the artist himself once said. On another occasion he wrote, "The art I dream of is an art of equilibrium, of purity and quiet joy." As the leader of the "Fauvists," Matisse accentuated the decorative and non-illusory pictorial aspects of his pictures, and in this way reached the "sense-intoxicated joy" of artistic creation. He also frequently concentrated a large number of studies, made with all kinds of media such as charcoal or stump, into one final pen-drawing, thickening the form as much as possible. This was the method he used for the expressive representations of the life he loved, in his own words, "with almost religious fervor." The drawing reproduced here seems almost classical in mood today, but it can certainly be designated as one of the masterpieces of modern graphic art.

HENRI MATISSE
FEMALE NUDE FROM THE BACK

(Le Cateau 1869—1954 Nice)
Female Nude from the Back
Pen and india ink · 42 x 31,2 cm · Private Collection

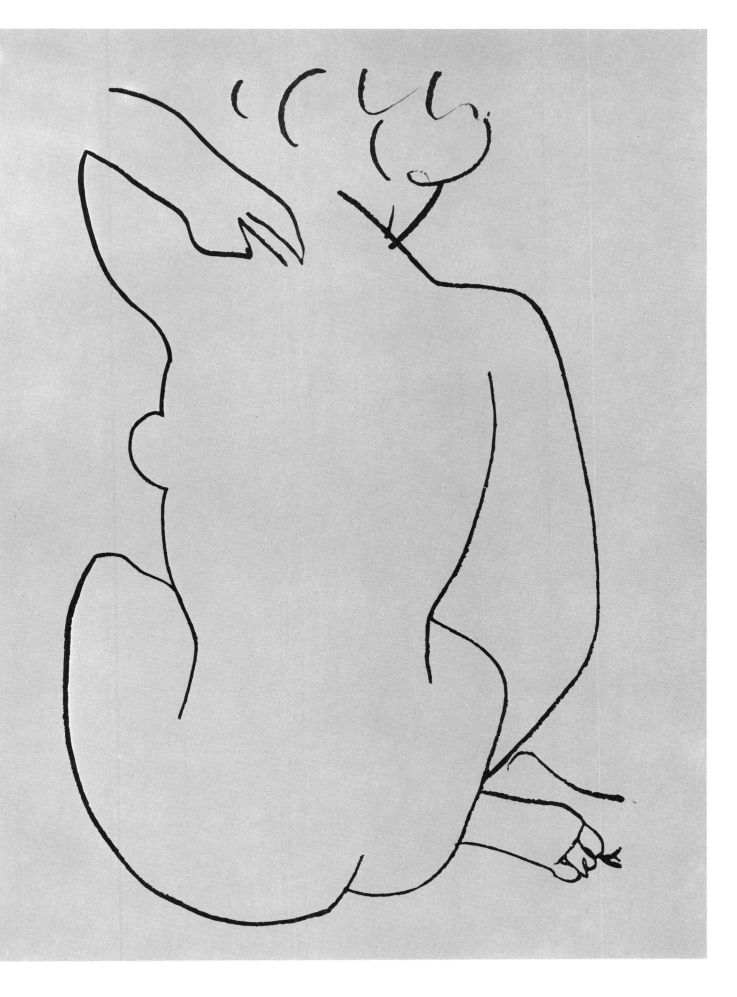

Narrow, gaunt shoulders, thin arms with long hands and bony fingers, dreaming or careworn faces — these are the characteristics of the girls and women that Picasso painted in Paris after 1900. His long series of scenes from the lives of jugglers and vagabonds alone would be enough to convince every critic of his later art that Picasso is a genius. Whether he used oils, water-color, gouache or pen, his sorrowful figures of that period, the so-called Blue Period, run counter to the traditional ideal of beauty. But they are always, unmistakably, the creatures of a superhuman imagination. Picasso, whose early pictures now command fortunes whenever they appear on the market, was suffering from hunger himself at the time. With a few striking lines that stand out from the umber, red and blue, the master unveils before our eyes the tragedy of the starving woman who fears for the fate of her child.

PABLO RUIZ Y PICASSO
MOTHER AND CHILD

*(Malaga 1881—) · Ink and water-color · 35,3 x 25,4 cm
Budapest, Szépmüvészeti Mùséum*

For the color pictures we are indebted to the following studios:

Beville, Philadelphia · Alfred Carlebach, London · Hermann Claasen, Cologne Giraudon, Paris · Gleixner, Munich · Photo Georges Groc, Toulouse · Hans Hinz, Basle · Walter Klein, Düsseldorf · Ralph Kleinhempel, Hamburg · Karl Meyer, Vienna · Mungenast und Reutlinger, Stuttgart · Preiss & Co., Ismaning Gerhard Reinhold, Leipzig · Umberto Rossi, Venice · Societa Scala, Florence Walter Steinkopf, Berlin

The reproduction rights for the pictures on page 23, 215, 219, 233, 235
were granted by
Cosmopress, Geneva and S P A D E M , Paris